Defence of Rev. B. T. Roberts, A. M. before the Genesee Conference of the Methodist Episcopal Church, at Perry, N. Y. Oct. 13-21, 1858

From notes and testimony taken at the trial by

Samuel K.J. Chesbrough

First Fruits Press
Wilmore, Kentucky
c2017

Defence of Rev. B. T. Roberts, A. M. before the Genesee Conference of the Methodist Episcopal Church, at Perry, N. Y. Oct. 13-21, 1858.
From notes and testimony taken at the trial by Samuel K.J. Chesbrough.

First Fruits Press, ©2017
Previously published by Clapp, Matthews & Co's Steam Printing House, 1858.

ISBN: 9781621716525 (print), 9781621716532 (digital), 9781621716549 (kindle)

Digital version at http://place.asburyseminary.edu/freemethodistbooks/28/

Chesbrough, Samuel K. J.
  Defence of Rev. B. T. Roberts, A. M. before the Genesee Conference of the Methodist Episcopal Church, at Perry, N. Y. Oct. 13-21, 1858 / from notes and testimony taken at the trial by Samuel K.J. Chesbrough.--Wilmore, Kentucky : First Fruits Press, ©2017.
        69 pages; 21 cm.
        Reprint. Previously published: Buffalo, [New York] : Clapp, Matthews & Co's Steam Printing House, 1858.
        ISBN 9781621716525 (pbk.)
        1. Roberts, Benjamin Titus, 1823-1893--Trials, litigation, etc. 2. Church controversies--Methodist Episcopal Church. 3. Free Methodist Church of North America--History. 4. Methodist Episcopal Church. Genesee Conference--History. I. Title. II. Methodist Episcopal Church. Genesee Conference.
BX8419.R6 C53 2017   287.2

Cover design by Jon Ramsay

asburyseminary.edu
800.2ASBURY
204 North Lexington Avenue
Wilmore, Kentucky 40390

First Fruits
THE ACADEMIC OPEN PRESS OF ASBURY SEMINARY

First Fruits Press
The Academic Open Press of Asbury Theological Seminary
204 N. Lexington Ave., Wilmore, KY 40390
859-858-2236
first.fruits@asburyseminary.edu
asbury.to/firstfruits

DEFENCE

OF

REV. B. T. ROBERTS, A. M.

BEFORE THE

GENESEE CONFERENCE

OF THE

METHODIST EPISCOPAL CHURCH,

AT PERRY, N. Y., OCT. 13—21, 1858.

"HE THAT JUDGETH ME IS THE LORD."—ST. PAUL.

FROM NOTES AND TESTIMONY TAKEN AT THE TRIAL,

BY SAMUEL K. J. CHESBROUGH.

BUFFALO:
CLAPP, MATTHEWS & CO'S STEAM PRINTING HOUSE.
OFFICE OF THE MORNING EXPRESS.
1858.

INTRODUCTION.

The difficulties of the Genesee Conference had their origin some years ago, in the connection of several of its more prominent preachers with the Odd Fellows and Masons. Many of the old and tried members of the Church remembered with horror the abduction and murder of Morgan; and they could not, in conscience, give their support to those Ministers who were in sympathy and fellowship with the perpetrators of that atrocious deed. Some, who refused to receive the sacraments at the hands of these secret society Ministers, or to contribute for their support, were, under various pretexts, cut off from the Church. Dissensions followed.

To check these evils a pamphlet, taking strong grounds against the connection of Methodist Ministers with secret societies, written by Rev. C. D. Burlingham, was circulated in the Conference, at its session in 1848, by Rev. Eleazer Thomas.

We give a single paragraph from this pamphlet, that the reader may see that the results recently realized were long since anticipated by far seeing men.

" It is believed that the *direct tendency* of Odd Fellowism is, the formation of parties in the *Conference,* in the *Church,* and in *Civil Society ;*—parties injurious to the cause of God and dangerous to the state. As all the operations and movements of the order are arranged in secret conclave, all persons except the initiated, are supposed to be ignorant of its nightly transactions. It must be well known, that a *small party,* acting in perfect *concert* and in *secret,* bound together by strong *partizan* feeling, and under the influence of an obligation imposed upon its members, deemed by them as *sacred* perhaps as an *oath*, is able to control, in almost any given case, a *multitude* of unsuspecting men, who are not under the influence of such affinities. And may we not justly fear, when a score or two of the members of our Conference, embracing the various *intellectual* grades in the Ministry, shall combine under such influences as above named, that a *favoritism* (if nothing more) will be practised, *on account of attachment to the "Order,"* which will create envyings and jealousies in the Ministry, and very much injure all the interests of the Church?"

This pamphlet caused at once a great commotion. The secret society men were wonderfully excited. Some, now occupying prominent positions in the church, said, if "they had to leave either, they would leave the Church before they would the Lodge." The conservatives were greatly alarmed. They begged the offended brethren not to "rend the Church in pieces." The secret society men were appeased by a "compromise" resolution ; which, as they construed it, conceded all they wished. They then learned a lesson which they have not been slow to profit by, that all they had to do to carry their points was to stand together and assume a threatening attitude, and enough "union savers" would rally to their support to give them a majority. Around this nucleus gathered those whose religious sympathies and experience led them to place dependence upon worldly policy for the advancement of the interests of the Church.

At the head of those opposed to this secret society worldly policy party, stood Rev. Eleazer Thomas. Around him rallied those who sympathized deeply with the doctrine of holiness as taught by the M. E. Church. After his transfer to California, the Lord raised up Revs. I. C. Kingsley, C. D. Burlingham, and L. Stiles to lead on his hosts ; the first for P. E. of Niagara District, the second of Olean, and the third of Genesee. Camp meetings, which had been revived, were kept up with increasing usefulness; Quarterly meetings, especially those known as "General· Quarterly Meetings," were attended with deep interest; and the work of full salvation went on with something of the primitive Methodist life and vitality.

At the Conference held two years since at Medina the secret society men, now known as the Buffalo regency, or regency party, to the number of some thirty, entered into a combination, threatening not to take work unless Kingsley and Stiles, who were very popular among the people, the latter especially, were removed from the Cabinet. Being satisfied that one or both of them would be removed, they asked for a transfer to the Cincinnati Conference, which was, unhesitatingly, granted. In their places were appointed men subservient to the wishes of the regency party. The P. E. of Genesee District at one of the first Quarterly meetings he held, entertained, put to vote, and allowed to pass and to be published as "Quarterly Conference Proceedings," a preamble and resolutions, condemning persons of the opposite party in their absence, who were not responsible to that tribunal.

At the Conference held in 1857 at LeRoy, an issue was made between the opposing parties, upon the election of the Secretary of the Conference. Rev. James M. Fuller was elected over Rev. B. T. Roberts, by some two or three majority.

Revs. I. C. Kingsley and L. Stiles, at the request of a large number of preachers and people, were re-transferred to the Genesee Conference. This occasioned a P. E. to say, "*If these men come back we are in for a seven year's war.*"

The " WAR " was commenced by presenting a bill of charges against Rev. B. T. Roberts, and two bills of charges against Rev. W. C. Kendall. That against the former was prosecuted, and voted sustained. Those against the latter were deferred for want of time, with the assurance that they would be prosecuted next year.

Kingsley, seeing how the battle was going, went back to the Cincinnati Conference. Notwithstanding these adverse influences, the cause of holiness advanced in the Conference more during the year than ever before. The camp meetings held in Genesee and Niagara districts, without the co-operation of the Presiding Elders, were the largest and most successful of any held in latter years in this region.

The regency party seemed to grow more and more desperate, and for months before Conference intimations were given out that those most prominent in getting up and sustaining these meetings must be expelled.   In the expressive, though not very elegant language of a regency preacher, " Nazaritism," the name given to Methodism in earnest, " must be crushed out; and WE HAVE GOT THE TOOLS TO DO IT WITH."

In the following pages you have an account of the means employed to carry this *holy* purpose into execution.

We have not published all the testimony—as some of it is merely cumulative, and some irrelevant—but we have given *all* that we conceive can have any bearing against the defendant. We desire that all should have the means of forming an impartial opinion in the case.   For ourselves, we doubt if a greater outrage has been perpetrated, under the forms of Ecclesiastical law, since the days of the Inquisition.

The regency party, by presenting an undivided front, have been able generally to screen one another, and to strike down an opponent they dreaded.   Thus, complaints made against some of their number for dishonesty of the most aggravated character, have been promptly dismissed, without an investigation, by the Conference.

A charge brought against the Rev. A. D. Wilbor, for the act of administration referred to, was promptly voted not to be entertained, though a more gross act of mal-administration can hardly be conceived.

To obtain their majority in the Conference, they have left no stone unturned.   The book-room influence, the superannuated fund, and the power of the presiding Eldership* have all been put into requisition. Help has also freely been imported from abroad. Thus at the last session, a P. E. of the Erie Conference, who has made himself quite officious in our troubles, left his district for nearly three weeks, and staid until the last head was taken off. A promising young preacher, who had served his two years of probation with acceptance to the Church, was about to be received, when this P. E. being called upon by one of the party, promptly stepped forward, and stated, apparently *con amore*, that he had heard some one say, that this young preacher, at a camp meeting held in this P. E.'s district, said " He thanked

---

* During the progress of the trial, T. Carlton was heard to say, " We can do nothing in this matter without the Presiding Elders, and them we will have."

God there was no P. E. present to steady the ark." *The young man was not admitted.*

We present this account of the defence of one of the champions of the cross in the fervent hope that good may result. We trust that the chief actors in the outrage, as well as the " tools " by which it was consummated, will, upon sober reflection, repent of, confess, and as far as possible, repair the wrong that they have done. We deem it due to the Church, and to the public, that they should know why the highest penalty known to Ecclesiastical law has been inflicted upon one who has stood prominently before them, and enjoyed their confidence.

CHARGES AND SPECIFICATIONS

AGAINST

BENJAMIN T. ROBERTS.

CHARGE.—*I hereby charge Benjamin T. Roberts with Unchristian and Immoral Conduct.*

SPECIFICATIONS.

First.—Contumacy: In disregarding the admonition of this Conference, in its decision upon his case at its last session.

Second.—In re-publishing, or assisting in the re-publishing and circulation of a document, entitled "New School Methodism," the original publication of which had been pronounced by this Conference unchristian and immoral conduct.

Third.—In publishing, or assisting in the publication and circulation of a document, printed in Brockport, and signed "George W. Estes," and appended to the one entitled "New School Methodism," and containing among other libels upon this Conference generally, and upon some of its members particularly, the following, to wit:

1.—"For several years past there has been the annual sacrifice of a human victim at the Conference."

2.—"No man is safe who dares even whisper a word against this secret inquisition in our midst."

3.—"Common crime can command its indulgencies; bankruptcies and adulteries are venal offenses; but opposition to its schemes and policies is a mortal sin—a crime without benefit of clergy."

4.—That "the same fifty men who voted Bro. Roberts guilty of unchristian and immoral conduct, voted to re-admit a Brother for the service performed of kissing a young lady."

5.—That " Bro. Roberts' trial was marked by gross iniquity of proceedings."

6.—That "on the trial a right which any civil or military court would have allowed him, was denied."

7.—That " a venerable Doctor of Divinity read the "*Auto-da-fe*" sermon, wherein he consigned in true Inquisitorial style, Bro. Roberts, body and soul, to hell."

8.—That "this venerable " D. D." is quite efficient in embarrassing effective preachers in their work, and pleading them to hell for the crime of preaching and writing the truth."

9.—That " there is a clique among us, called the Buffalo Regency, conspiring and acting in secret conclave, to kidnap, or drive away, or proscribe and destroy, by sham trials and starvation appointments, every one who has the boldness to question their supremacy in the Conference."

10.—That "the fearless champions of true Methodism are being cloven down one after another in our sight."

11.—That "the aforesaid members of this Conference are a " monster power," which is writhing its slimy folds around the Church of God and crushing out its life."

Perry, Oct. 11, 1858.   Signed :

DAVID NICHOLS.

At the request of the complainant, Rev. James M. Fuller was appointed to assist in the prosecution ; subsequently Rev. Thomas Carlton was added.

The defendant asked that he might be permitted to have as counsel a member of another Annual Conference. Bishop Janes decided, Bishop Baker concurring, that he could not go out of this Conference for counsel. He then requested that Bro. Ives might, with his consent, be transferred to this Conference to assist defendant in this trial.

Bishop Janes decided that the right to make a transfer grew out of the right to make appointments. He could not therefore make a transfer for the purpose desired.

Rev. L. Stiles was appointed to assist in the defense.

The defendant offered, if the complaint would be withdrawn, and the action be removed to a Civil Court where an oath could be administered, and witnesses be compelled to testify, to give good security for the payment of all costs and damages that might be recovered against him. He requested that the offer might go upon the Journal. The offer was declined and the request refused.

The defendant asked that the venue might be changed to another Conference, and that he might be transferred to the Oneida Conference for this purpose.

In support of this request Mr. Roberts spoke in substance as follows:

"Mr. PRESIDENT : The request that I have made may be an unusual one, but I trust you will see that it is not unreasonable. I am entirely willing to meet everything that I have done, but I claim that I am entitled to a fair and impartial trial. It is a wise provision of the law of the land, that "the venue may be changed to another County, when the defendant conceives he cannot have a fair and impartial trial in the County where the venue is laid."—Burrill's Practice, p. 141. Such is the state of party feeling in this Conference, that a fair and impartial trial is entirely out of the question. It cannot be had. Men have ceased to act from the convictions of their own judgment ; the voice of justice cannot be heard amid the clamor of partizan strife. The party opposed to me, by threatening to make disturbance, have obtained the control of four out of five of the districts; this has given them a clear majority in the Conference. Questions are not decided according to their merits, but according to their party bearings. Their secret meetings keep them together; as the leaders go, all go.

Thus, during the trial at the last session, a motion made by a friend of mine was promptly voted down by the regency party. One of their leaders then renewed the motion, and said a few words to the effect that the motion was about the thing. No additional light was shed upon the question. The same men voted for it that, but a few moments before, raised their hands against it. So, during the present session, upon the question of the admission into full connection of a brother who is supposed to belong to our side of the house, the vote was taken and he was rejected by the usual majority. Before the Bishop had time to announce the decision, a brother obtained the floor, and re-opened the discussion. Meanwhile the leaders of the regency came

in, and said they should go for him; they brought forward no
new facts or reasons, but up went all hands in his favor. We
have seen so much of this, that we cannot forbear applying to
them the words of Cowper:

> " With packhorse constancy they keep the road,
> Crooked or straight, o'er quags or thorny dells,
> True to the jingling of their leaders' bells."

A matter of this magnitude should never be allowed to be
settled according to the preponderance of this or that party. It
is of more importance that justice should be done, than that
precedents should be followed.

I should not be at all surprised if this trial had already been
decided in the secret meetings of those who comprise a majority
of the Conference. I know it will be denied; it has been repeatedly denied that my case was prejudged last year.

Yet I have been recently told by a member of the regency
party, that he had no idea that any charges would have been
presented against me last year, had they not felt satisfied, from
action taken in their secret meetings, that my condemnation
would be secured. Sir, I am not willing to be tried by men
who are capable of pursuing such a course. Their decision cannot command respect.

I look upon this whole matter, last year and this, as a wanton
persecution. It is deemed necessary to the success of the party
to injure my standing, and cripple my influence to the fullest
extent possible.

I had nothing to do, whatever, with writing or publishing the
pamphlet signed G. W. Estes. It was written and published
without my knowledge or consent. It contains some things that
I never approved of. It went into circulation without my agency.
Had I been in my grave, it would probably have been circulated
more extensively than it has been. If there is any crime involved in this circulation, most of the preachers in the Conference
have been equally guilty with myself. I am willing to bear my
own sins, but I do not consent to be made a scape-goat, to bear
the sins of this Conference.

Whoever I should be tried by, if at all, I certainly should not
be by them. Everything indicates that an occasion is sought.
It is time that a stop was put to these partizan prosecutions."

The chair decided that a transfer for the purpose of a trial could not be made. "The discipline makes preachers responsible to the Conferences to which they belong."

The defendant then asked that he might be tried by a committee, according to the provision of the discipline. Part I, Ch. X. § 2, p. 93.

He said, "Mr. President: Since I cannot be tried by impartial and unprejudiced men, it seems to me that I have a right to ask to be tried by a committee, so small that each man composing it will feel a high degree of personal responsibility for the decision he may make. It is well known that men often do in a body what they would scorn to do as individuals. They hide themselves in each other's shadow. Socrates was wont to say, that though every man in Athens were a philosopher, an Athenian assembly would still be little better than a mob. In large bodies reason and judgment often give place to party zeal and prejudice. I would rather be tried by a committee composed entirely of men of the opposite side, than by the Conference in its present condition. I would be willing to leave it to the presiding Elders, though all but one are opposed to us. I would have the trial go on now, in just as public a manner as though it were before the entire Conference.

Another reason why this case should not go before the Conference is this: It is alleged that some members of this body are specially injured in their individual character by the publication complained of. They have, then, a deep personal interest in the issue of this trial. Though they do not appear in the complaint, yet they are, in reality, parties in the case.

Now, sir, it is, I believe, a well established principle, prevailing wherever the right of trial by jury prevails, that no one can sit as judge or juror in a case in which he is personally interested. It has been decided that if a positive statute should give this right, such enactment would be null and void.

"If the law say that a man shall be a judge in his own cause, such law being contrary to natural equity, shall be void, for 'jura naturae sunt immutabilia.' They are leges legum." That is, "Natural rights," are immutable. They are the laws of laws. Hobart's report, page 87, Day vs. Savage.

This, sir, is the equitable provision of the common law; and shall the plainest principles of justice be set aside in an Ecclesiastical investigation? Here, if anywhere, we ought to look for the most perfect impartiality. Every precaution should be taken, that can be taken, to have the question settled according to its merits. But if the Conference decides it, it will be, I am satisfied, by a party vote. My request is certainly reasonable. If brethren wish me to have anything like a fair trial they cannot refuse it."

James M. Fuller opposed letting the case go before a committee. He said "a committee would be as partizan as the Conference. Is it true that this body of professed Ministers are so actuated by party zeal that a fair trial cannot be had?"

A. Kendall: "Can we do less than grant the request of Bro. Roberts? Nine or twelve old members would certainly give a more judicious and impartial verdict than the Conference, in the present state of party feeling."

Dr. Lucky: "I am in favor of having this case go to a committee. It should have gone to one in the first place. It never ought to have been brought here in its present form."

H. Ryan Smith: "You cannot find nine or fifteen men who will be willing to take the responsibility of deciding this case. They would feel crushed under it. I do not believe that a majority of this Conference can be brought to do wrong. Party lines are clearly drawn, yet I mean to do right."

T. Carlton: "Reference has been made to secret meetings, and the trial of last year. I did not attend a secret meeting at Le Roy. We had select meetings, but there were no votes taken to condemn Bro. Roberts. The vote was that Bro. Roberts should have a fair trial. Reflections have been made upon this Conference. The trial should be public, in this Church. It should not go to a committee."

B. T. Roberts: "I have stated that I wanted the trial to be public; I do most earnestly. I should be unwilling to have it go to a committee if it could not be just as public as though the entire Conference should vote upon the case. If it goes before a committee they will feel bound to listen patiently to the testimony, and examine the case. If the Conference proceed to try it, many of the members will, I fear, do as some did last year, be absent while the testimony is being taken, but be on hand to vote without having heard the evidence which should control their votes.* I am sorry to hear it repeatedly said by brethren of the other side, that they had no secret meetings at Le Roy. What do they mean? How can they hazard such assertions? I will read the minutes of one of these meetings. They came into my hands providentially, in an honorable manner; but how, no one will know.

"Le Roy, September 3d, 1857.

Meeting convened according to adjournment, Bro. Parsons in the chair. Prayer by Bro. Fuller.

Brethren present pledged themselves by rising, to keep to themselves the proceedings of this meeting.

Moved, that we will not allow the character of B. T. Roberts to pass, until he has had a fair trial.—Passed.

Moved, that we will not pass the character of Rev. W. C. Kendall, until he has had a fair trial.—Passed.

Moved, that Bro. Carlton be added to the committee on Bro. Kendall's case.—Passed."

Thus, it seems that secret meetings were really held. This secret Conclave assumed to act in a judicial manner upon the cases of absent brethren. The promise to give them "a fair trial," means the same as the promise of the Administration to give the people of Kansas a fair election, under border ruffian sway. What right had this Conclave to say that any Brother should have a trial at all?

Their action rendered "a fair trial" impossible. Thus you see I have good reason for not wishing to be tried by these men. Give me a committee."

C. D. BURLINGHAM: "This is a solemn hour; the results of this trial will not end with the session of this body. After the adjournment of the last Conference, I learned some facts in regard to the secret meetings, and the action had in them in Bro. Roberts' case, that astounded me. I think we ought to grant his request; fifteen impartial men can be found. The provision of the discipline, authorizing a committee, was made by the last General Conference, for the very purpose of meeting such cases. The Conference should grant the request."

* This was actually the case. While the examination of witnesses was going on, some of the preachers were away in the woods gathering chesnuts, others were lounging about the door, and in the lecture room. But care was taken to have them present in time to vote.

S. C. Church : "There is not one of us but supposes an impartial trial can be had by a committee. These brethren say they do not think they can have a fair trial before the Conference. They are honest in this conviction. I ask in the name of our holy religion, do they not make a reasonable request? How shall we suffer? how will the Church suffer, by our permitting this case to go before a committee? Bro. Roberts has been tried by us once; he feels afflicted about that trial. Let us grant his request."

Dr. Chamberlayne : "In regard to an impartial trial, would not a committee partake of the partizan character of the Conference? The vote for Secretary stood 34 to 63. What of the 34? Are they not prejudiced? I suppose no one doubts but that the 63 are prejudiced. Whence then can fifteen impartial men be found?"

Dr. Luckey : "I think the case should by all means go to a committee."

The vote was taken with the following result: In favor of referring the case to a committee, 39. Against such reference, 48. So the request for a committee was denied.

The defendant then entered the following objection. "I object to any member of this Conference sitting upon this trial as a juror, who feels himself *personally*, in his individual character, libelled by the article complained of. I also object to any person sitting upon this trial as juror, who has taken any action, or participated in any action, upon the case, in any secret or public meeting, or who has expressed an opinion in regard to the merits of the case."

Decision by Bishop Janes. "Bro. Roberts has requested the chair to exclude from the Conference during the trial, those members who claim to be specially and individually libelled in the article complained of in the specifications.

Our answer is: The chair does not organize or appoint this Court. The discipline appoints it. And whatever may be our convictions in the case, we judge we have no authority to say that any member of the Conference shall not sit or vote."

TESTIMONY TAKEN ON THE TRIAL.

I.—In Relation to the Publication of the Pamphlet signed Geo. W. Estes.

GEORGE W. ESTES called.—Bro. Roberts had nothing to do with publishing or assisting in publishing the document under consideration,* to my knowledge, and I presume to know. He had nothing to do with the writing of the part that bears my name; I do not know that he had any knowledge that its publication was intended; he never gave his consent that the part entitled "New School Methodism," should be re-published by me or any one else to my knowledge; he was never responsible for the payment of its publication, in whole or in part; he never contributed any thing to the expenses of its publication to my knowledge; I intended that so far as sold, it should go to defray expenses of publication; I never sold any to him.

Cross Examination.—I never forwarded or caused to be forwarded any of them to Bro. Roberts; I never gave any to him personally; I do not know of any one giving or forwarding him any. I never gave orders to any one to forward Bro. R. any, to my knowledge.

Rev. A. D. WILBOR called.—I am acquainted with George W. Estes. He is an exhorter in our Church. The last quarterly Conference at Clarkson renewed his license, and I signed it. I have never circulated any of the Pamphlets.†

II.—Circulation of the Pamphlet.

Rev. JOHN BOWMAN called.—I have seen this document entitled "New School Methodism," and "To whom it may concern," signed George W. Estes, before. I first saw it on the Cars, between Medina and Lockport. Bro. Roberts presented it to me; several were presented in a package; there were, I think, three dozen. Bro. Roberts desired me to leave a portion of them at Medina, conditionally. He requested me to circulate them; he desired me to leave a portion of them with Bro. Codd, or Bro. Williams of Medina, provided I fell in company with them; I put a question to him whether they were to be distributed gratuitously, or sold. He said he would like to get enough to defray the expense of printing, but circulate them any-

---

* See document A. Appendix.

† How could Rev. A. D. Wilbor license George W. Estes as an exhorter, *knowing that he published the Pamphlet*, and yet lend his influence, and give his vote for the expulsion of members of the Conference, for simply circulating it? His effort to make the quarterly Conference responsible, is no credit to his intelligence. He ought to know that the Presiding Elder renews exhorters' licenses, with the approbation of the quarterly Conference. The recommendation of the quarterly Conference does not render it obligatory upon him, to renew the license of an exhorter. See Dis. Part I, Ch. IV, Page 11—Page 66.

2

how; he desired me not to make it known that he had any agency in the matter of circulating the document, if I could consistently keep it to myself. I do not know where Bro. R. got on the Cars; my impression is, we were traveling east. I do not know as anything more was said about the payment of printing them; my recollection is not very distinct; he mentioned he had been at some considerable expense.

Cross Examination.—I was counsel for defendant last year; he appeared to repose confidence in me; the conversation referred to on the Cars was between the last of October and the last of November, 1857; it was after I moved; I told him I would take the documents, and consider the case. I took them directly to my house; I put them away in a by-place; all of them; I did not show them to any body till more then six months after I received them; about six weeks ago, I let Dr. Chamberlayne have one; Dr. C. took several copies; I lent them to him; I can not say whether he has returned them or not; I think I have showed them to others, I am not positive. I do not recollect to have read a copy to any person. I cannot tell how many copies passed out of my hand, very few. I never read this document in public.

Rev. S. M. HOPKINS called by defence.—I have read the Pamphlet signed George W. Estes, put in as testimony; I have had several numbers of copies in my possession; I have had twenty-six; I bought some, some were presented to me. I decline answering what I did with them on account of charges preferred against me.

Rev. RUSSEL WILCOX called.—I am a local deacon of the M. E. Church in Pekin. I am intimately acquainted with Bro. Roberts, the Pastor of the Church in Pekin. I do not know that he has ever circulated this pamphlet anywhere; I first saw it after I left home, on my way to this Conference.

Rev. J. P. KENT called.—I did ask the defendant for one of these Pamphlets. I wished to see one of them, and I asked Bro. Roberts if he could let me have one; he said he did not circulate them, but had no objection to my seeing the one that he had. This was a few weeks ago, at the Holly or Albion grove meeting; perhaps it was about the 1st of August.

III.—IN RELATION TO THE SECRET MEETINGS HELD BY THE PARTY KNOWN AS THE "BUFFALO REGENCY."

Rev. SANFORD HUNT called.—I was at the Medina Conference: Bros. Stiles and Kingsley were Presiding Elders during the year preceding that Conference; I may not be aware of all the measures that were taken to have them removed; I saw a petition to Bishop Morris to that effect; I do not know where it was got up; I am not certain where I saw it first; I think I saw it first in front of the Church; I cannot tell. I was present at meetings at the house of John Ryan; the subject of their fitness for the office was discussed; some brethren felt aggrieved at their administration. The matter was talked of by some men that they did not feel safe, as Methodist preachers, in the hands of these two Presiding Elders; I cannot tell how far the matter was talked over; I do not know of any one threatening to leave the Conference; they did not to my knowledge threaten to leave the Church. I heard some say that they would not take work, and then they withdrew the statement; I am not certain whether they withdrew it at the meeting in which they made it or not. It is possible I may have given my opinion that certain ones would leave if their wishes were not complied with; I think there were over thirty names on that petition. I think Bro. Stiles' trial was talked of, but have no recollection; I think there was a chairman and secretary at that meeting; there were generally twenty or thirty at the meeting; we had about three meetings; do not know who was chairman; if I did should decline to tell.

Rev. W. C. WILLING called.—I did not act as door keeper for any meeting in Medina; I stood outside the door of all the Churches at Medina, and outside of one or two, while meetings were being held within. I did not stay outside all the time. The meetings were purely of a religious character; they were all composed mainly of preachers; some of those meetings were composed exclusively of males; the one at the Presbyterian Church. I should think the most of the Conference were at one of them. I was present at another, composed of a smaller number at the same Church. My impression is that I invited Bro. Stiles to go in. I had no official connection with that meeting. If I made the remark, "I am acting as door keeper," I do not recollect it. There was a meeting at the Presbyterian Church, called by Bro. J. G. Miller, for the purpose of securing a union for a better state of things among us. Bro. Miller invited me to come, and invite my friends. I did so, I think I invited Bro. Stiles.

Cross Examination.—The meetings referred to were not secret. I did not attend any secret meetings during the session of the Medina Conference. I attended meetings of Brethren and Sisters, at the house of John Ryan; *we ate of his excellent peaches.* We talked there about Conference matters, and prayed fervently over them, different Brethren in the ministry at different times leading in prayer. I was there three times only.

Direct Examination resumed.—About how many prayers did you have at a meeting?

ANS.—Just as many as there were persons there.

QUES.—Do you mean to be understood that every person present led in prayer?

ANS.—No.

QUES.—How many led at each meeting?

ANS.—My recollection is not distinct whether we had more than one season or not, of prayer.

QUES.—How many persons led in prayer at each season of prayer?

ANS.—That is a question I cannot definitely answer. If I could I would.

QUES.—Was there any more than simply a prayer offered at the beginning and close of these meetings?

ANS.—While we were at those meetings, we had seasons of prayer, and we all engaged in prayer; it was a time of prayerful interest and kindliest feelings. My impression is that there was not more than two leading prayers at any one meeting. There was, I think, a chairman and a secretary at those meetings. The continuance of Bro. Stiles and Kingsley, in the P. E. Office, was talked of. My impression is that the superannuated Ministers were talked of. There was no notice publicly given of these meetings. I was present at select meetings at the Le Roy Conference; they were held over Bryant's store; I think there was a chairman at those meetings. I could not say positively who was chairman; I think Bro. Parsons; I have not the slightest recollection who was secretary. The case of Wm. C. Kendall was brought before the meeting. There were laymen present who pressed the subject upon the attention of the meeting. According to my best recollection no action was had by the Minister upon the subject. The sentiment was advanced in reply to the representation of the laymen, that we were not there to discuss preachers' characters. *I think the name of Bro. B. T. Roberts was mentioned there.* A. D. Wilbor's name was mentioned. I have been present at select meetings at the present session of our Conference.

Cross Examination Resumed—Questions by Thomas Carlton.

QUES.—Bro. Willing, at those meetings at Medina were the Spiritual interests of the Church freely talked of, and suggestions made as to the best means of promoting revivals of Religion?

ANS.—They were.

QUES.—Was the necessity of enforcing the rules of our discipline talked of?

ANS.—It was.

QUES.—What was the opinion expressed as to the means to be used to promote Spiritual Religion, and the enforcement of the rules of discipline?

ANS.—There was a hearty and unanimous expression of love to the Church, and to the cause of God.

QUES.—Were the same subjects talked of, and the same feeling expressed at those meetings held at Le Roy?

ANS.—They were.

QUES.—Was anything said at these meetings at Medina or Le Roy about its being unsafe for any members of the Conference to disagree with the views held by the members of that meeting, or anything to that effect?

ANS.—Nothing of the kind that I can recall.

QUES.—Did you ever hear in any of those meetings, (I embrace all,) any threats of proscription, or that of any being sent to starvation or hard appointments?

ANS.—I heard nothing of the kind.

QUES.—By T. Carlton: Were there any inquisitorial powers exercised in those meetings? Objection by defendant.

B. T. ROBERTS.—Mr. President: I object to the question as improper, for the reason that if answered it would make the witness a judge of opinions, and not a narrator of facts. Let the witness tell what did take place, and then it will be for the Court to decide, and not for the witness, whether such action is "inquisitorial" or not. His opinion as to what is "inquisitorial" and ours may differ. Let the witness give the facts that took place.

THOMAS CARLTON.—Mr. President: I insist that the question shall be answered. It is perfectly proper. We are charged with having exercised "inquisitorial powers," and we want the witness to say whether we did or not. If a man was charged with murder, it would be perfectly proper to ask the witness whether he saw the murder committed or not.

B. T. ROBERTS.—Mr. President: I am surprised to hear one occupying the position of the counsel, making such remarks. If a person were on trial for murder, the witness would be asked, not if he saw the murder committed, but what did he see done, that led to the death of the victim; and then it would be for the Court to determine whether such action constituted murder, manslaughter, or justifiable homicide.

Question waived.

Rev. D. F. PARSONS called.—I was chairman of these meetings held at Le Roy; there was a person who kept brief minutes of the meetings; I do not know whether he was called secretary or not. I do not recollect whether there was a committee on the case of William C. Kendall, or not. There was conversation before the meeting concerning Bro. Kendall; I think the brethren pledged themselves by a rising vote, to keep to themselves the proceedings of the meetings; I do not remember a motion or vote that we will not let the character of B. T. Roberts pass until he has a fair trial; I do not remember as his case was before the meeting in form of a motion; there was consultation concerning his case, and the general sentiment, so far as expressed, was, that he should have a fair trial; I do not recollect as a committee was appointed on his case; I do not recollect as any motion was passed, relative to Bro. Kendall; I do not know whether there were any charges present; I saw none.

Cross Examination—Questions by Thomas Carlton.

QUES.—Was the case of Wm. C. Kendall introduced before the meeting by a minister or layman?

ANS.—I think it was a layman on his charge.

QUES.—Were the Spiritual interests of the Church talked over in all the meetings you attended, both in Medina and Le Roy, and suggestions made as to the best means to be used to promote revivals of Religion?

ANS.—Some of those meetings were seasons of great Spiritual interest.

QUES.—Was the subject of enforcing the rules of the discipline in regard to the class meetings and love feasts, talked over, particularly at Medina?

ANS.—I do remember one such conversation.

QUES.—Was there unanimity among the brethren composing that meeting as to the means of promoting Spiritual Religion, and the work of holiness among the people?

ANS.—I discovered no difference of sentiment among those present.

QUES.—Was there agreement in favor of earnest piety and holiness as held and taught by the Methodist Church?

ANS.—Certainly.

QUES.—Did you discover in any of those meetings anything like proscription, or hear any threats made in reference to any who might disagree with any of us on any subject?

ANS.—Not to my recollection.

Direct Examination resumed.—Question by L. Stiles.

Was the most of the time in those meetings occupied in consultation as to promoting the Spirituality of the Church, and the enforcement of the discipline, or was most of the time occupied in other matters?

ANS.—My judgment is, that as much of the time was spent in considering those things which pertain to the peace and prosperity of the Church, as when we are in Conference.

Rev. THOMAS CARLTON called.—I attended three of the meetings at the house of John Ryan during the session of the Medina Conference. I attended some of the select meetings at Le Roy, not all. * * * * My impression is that at one of our meetings there was a person, either layman or preacher, I do not recollect which, not a member of our Conference, who was spoken to by a brother and requested to leave, because we were talking of Conference matters, and it was not proper he should be with us. He spoke to him and they went out. I should think there might have been 60 at one of those meetings, at another, about 40; they ranged from 30 to 60.

IV.—PROSCRIPTION AND THREATENINGS.

Rev. ALFRED KENDALL called.—I have heard remarks made about sacrificing, or expelling the defendant and some of his friends. The remarks of this kind that are most distinct in my mind were made previous to the session at Le Roy. We were talking about our Conference matters, especially about the course pursued by certain men, who were regarded as leading Nazarites. *The individual remarked that those men must be sacrificed*, and they would be; stating that he knew the views and feelings of leading men in this Conference, and also of Bishops. That was the substance of remarks bearing upon that point; the defendant was one of those about whom the conversation was being had; I am not competent to say whether the person I was conversing with is regarded as a leading man of the other party or not. I have always understood that he was identified with what is known as the Regency party; from his remarks I should conclude this to be the fact.

Cross Examination.—I have no knowledge of any organization, known as Buffalo Regency; all I know is by common report; I heard the term, Buffalo Regency, used at the Olean Conference; I cannot state distinctly whether I first heard it there or not; I have heard it frequently since the Olean Conference.

QUES.—Will you give us the name of the person with whom you had the conversation previous to the Le Roy Conference? Objected to by Defendant. Objection overruled. Chair decided the question should be answered.

ANS.—It was Bro. Gilbert De La Matyr. This conversation was, if my memory is not at fault, in the village of Attica, during the session of the preachers' district meeting in that place; I think the subject of conversation was, preachers holding meetings off from their own charges.

QUES.—Did you not have a pretty free conversation with him as to certain irregularities of certain members of this Conference?

ANS.—We had a free conversation, but I think it did not turn upon that point.

QUES.—Did not this brother say that these men must be expelled, or sacrificed, if they did not change their course?

ANS.—I have no recollection of any such remark; I am pretty sure that he used the word sacrificed; I am quite sure. I am not sure that the defendant's name was mentioned in the immediate connection with the word sacrificed; names were used during the conversation; remarks were made in regard to meetings held by Bro. Roberts and others; no individuals were particularly designated by name, as the subjects to be sacrificed, but they were understood from the tenor of the conversation; I am not certain that any other persons were present. Nothing more was said about the Bishops than I have mentioned; they were brought in incidentally. This conversation was not about what some regarded as the evils of Nazaritism. Reference was made to the removal of the P. Elders referred to, and its influence in confirming the Nazarites in the belief that those opposed to them were determined to get control of the appointments of Conference. Bro. D. did not say that those with whom he was in sympathy, were trying to get control of the Conference. I understood the sacrifice to mean, *the removal of those men from the Conference.*

Rev. WM. BARRET called.—I saw at the Medina Conference a petition asking for the removal of Bros. Stiles and Kingsley from the office of Presiding Elders; I did not go to a secret meeting; I cannot state the wording of the petition, but understood it to be this, that we would refuse to take work if Bros. Stiles and Kingsley were continued in the Presiding Elder's office.

Cross Examination.—I saw the petition in the basement of the M. E. Church, in Medina; I read some of it, and not all of it; I could not give a sentence verbatim; I did not read a sentence stating that we would not take work, but that was the understanding of those who signed; that was my understanding, and also of the brother who presented it. I cannot give a sentence verbatim; that was my understanding.

Rev. J. M. FULLER called.—QUES.—Did you state at the Medina Conference that you would not take work under either Bro. Stiles or Kingsley ?

ANS.—I did.

QUES.—Did you hear any one else say the same?

ANS.—I heard others say what would amount to about the same.

JESSE MURDOCK called.—I am a member of the M. E. Church in West Carlton. I had a conversation with a member of this Conference, and he said that three or four would probably have to be turned out ; in the course of conversation the names of McCreary and Roberts were mentioned ; we were talking about the camp meeting, and matters and things, and he thought this would put a stop to the difficulty ; he said this expelling them would put a stop to the trouble ; I think he said some would be expelled ; he wanted to know if I would go with them ; this conversation was a short time before the Bergen camp meeting.

Cross Examination.—The name of the brother with whom I had the conversation was A. Plumley ; I do not know that he based his opinion on anything that might take place after that.

J. W. REDDY called.—Bro. Plumley said he thought there would be a secession ; that if two or three of the leading men upon the Nazarite side were expelled from Conference, a portion of the people would go with them, and that they would be expelled if there was not a compromise or settlement of the difficulty in some way.

Cross Examination.—I took whatever he did say merely as his opinion ; I said I thought they would not be expelled ; he thought they would be, if there was not a compromise. His word was that they "would be" if there was not a compromise. I took it as his opinion.

Dr. CHAMBERLAYNE called.—I presented before the session of the Olean Conference, information touching a variety of things in the official conduct of Bro. McCreary, during the then closing year, in Yates station, which I believed was due to the Conference, in order to a just disposition of his case ; this was done partly in the way of oral statement, but mainly from minutes prepared for that purpose. At the Medina Conference my personal recollection is indistinct, as to my agency in preferring charges against Bro. Stiles ; but I am satisfied of the fact by a reference to the journal of my agency in the presentation of charges. I have no doubt but that I presented charges against Bro. Stiles, by referring to the journal. During the year following the Olean Conference I authorized charges against Bro. McCreary ; I signed them.

Rev. J. C. NOBLES called.—QUES.—What Conference do you belong to ?

ANS.—East Genesee.

QUES.—Did you belong to this Conference at the time it met at Medina ?

ANS.—I did.

QUES.—Will you state what you know about the means and measures that were employed to remove Stiles and Kingsley from the Cabinet.

ANS.—I have no knowledge, only what came from the Bishop ; I foolishly tried to keep Bro. K. in, and have regretted it ever since.

QUES.—Did you consider him fit to fill the office of Presiding Elder ?

ANS.—I did consider him competent until I found him to be a Nazarite, then I did not.

QUES.—What about Stiles?

ANS.—If I knew he was one, I should have the same opinion of him as of the other.

V.—REBUTTING TESTIMONY CALLED BY PROSECUTION.

Rev. GILBERT DE LA MATYR called.—I signed a remonstrance at the Medina Conference against the return of Bro. Kingsley to the district, for reasons which I stated to Bro. Kingsley in Conference at Medina: First, for things written to me in communications I had received from him. Next reason was, because being avowedly opposed to the distinctive features of Nazaritism, he (K.) supported that system politically.

QUES.—Will you state any particular thing referred to in those letters? Objected to; question withdrawn.

Recalled.—I was present this morning and heard the testimony of Bro. Kendall; I cannot detail the conversation referred to; this much I know, however, I never connected the Bishop's name with leading men in this Conference with the sacrificing of members of this Conference; I could not have related so glaring and foolish a falsehood without remembering it; there may have been conversation upon our Conference difficulties, which led Bro. Kendall to mistake in this matter at this distance of time; in this conversation I spoke not for a party but for myself.

Cross Examination.—QUES.—Do you remember distinctly anything that was said in that conversation?

ANS.—I do not.

Rev. JOHN BOWMAN called.—QUES.—Were you present at the Medina Conference?

ANS.—Yes.

QUES.—Do you remember making a speech on the floor of Conference in favor of Bro. Kingsley?

ANS.—In reply to some remarks I stated he was not entirely destitute of some things that might be praiseworthy.

QUES.—Did any one come to you out of Conference and say, you must take back what you said in his *favor, or you would rue it?*

ANS.—It appears I was misunderstood in my remarks; after my explanations it was made satisfactory.

QUES.—Was any threat made to you?

ANS.—I cannot say that there was.

QUES.—What did this person say would be the consequence, in case you had not taken it back?

ANS.—That the Conference might get a wrong impression as to the efficiency of Bro. Kingsley.

QUES.—What did he say would be the consequence to you personally?

ANS.—We should all suffer in common, in consequence of having an inefficient Presiding Elder.

Rev. A. PLUMLEY called.—Did you hear the testimony of Bro. Murdock?

ANS.—I did.

QUES.—Will you please state the substance of the conversation you had with him on the occasion referred to.

ANS.—I met Bro. Murdock some time in June, I think the fore part, before the Bergen camp meeting. He asked me if I was going to that camp meeting; I told him I was not able to go; I was then very unwell, weighed only 93 pounds, hardly able to stand up; told him I was not able to enter into that general conversation; he said he thought I was in favor of camp meetings; I told him I was, for I had been every year for seven years, some years twice; he then went into a general argument on the propriety of the Bergen camp meeting; said the people were with those who appointed them—justified them in that act; I told him that it was my opinion that Bros. Roberts and McCreary, and I think I said others, would lead off in a secession, that was my opinion; he say that they would do no such thing; I then said, Bro. M., suppose that these men, referring to Bro. R. and McC., should be expelled at the next Conference—I know nothing about it, but suppose they should—would you leave the Church? His reply was: I cannot say what I should do six months hence. This is about the amount of the conversation; I never said to any one that three or four would be expelled at this Conference. At a conversation some weeks subsequent, I said to Bro. Williams, a steward in my charge, after a long conversation on our Conference difficulties, I thought we should never have peace in our Conference till those men were removed.

Cross Examination.—I never said that Bros. Roberts, McCreary and Hard must be expelled; I never said that any one would be expelled. In connection with the other remark, that we would not have peace until their removal, I think I added, if that was the only thing that would settle our troubles, the sooner we were separated the better; I said nothing about they must be expelled.

VI.—Rebutting Testimony called by Defence.

Rev. WM. BARRET called.—Will you state what you heard Bro. Bowman state, at or soon after the Medina Conference, one of the members of this Conference said to him would be the result if he did not take back what he had said in favor of Kingsley? Objected to on the ground he had called a witness to rebut the testimony of his own witness. Defence stated that he was ready to offer it at the time, but was refused.

Chair decided the question to be proper.

Ans.—He said he had been threatened if he did not take back what he had said in favor of Kingsley on the Conference floor; that is the substance of his remark.

Rev. R. E. THOMAS called.—Bro. Bowman told me at the Medina Conference that a member of this Conference said to him, that if he did not take back what he had said in reference to Bro. Kingsley on the Conference floor, he would rue it; I think that was the expression; am not positive.

Cross Examination.—Am positive it was a member of this Conference that Bro. Bowman named to me, and not a layman.

Rev. S. C. CHURCH called.—Bro. Bowman said to me that a certain member of the Conference, at the Medina session, said to him, that if he would go before the Conference and take back what he said in Bro. Kingsley's favor, he might expect fair weather or a pleasant time; if not, he could give him no assurance of what would take place, or would transpire; that is as near as I can recollect; he said it was made by a member of this Conference, and he named the man.

Rev. E. S. FURMAN called.—Bro. Bowman said to me at the Medina Conference, that a certain member of the Conference told him that if he did not take back what he had said in favor of Bro. Kingsley, that he would rue it, or words to that effect.

Cross Examination.—Did the threat originate with a layman, a member of his Church at Medina?

ANS.—My impression is that it did not, but I could not say what these threats were.

Direct Examination resumed.—I heard nothing about the preacher's making this threat was under the authority of a layman, in this connection, at this time.

VII.—CONCERNING THE NAZARITES.

[Though the following testimony has no bearing upon the case, yet we have thought it best to publish it, that it may be seen how utterly without foundation is the report, that there is any such organization or association as the "Nazarite Society." It will be seen that such an association was merely proposed by one person, but was never formed. That two or three private caucuses have been held at different times, by those called Nazarites, under no pledge of secrecy.]

Rev. JAMES M. FULLER called.—I do not know of two parties in this Conference that have specific names; I have heard the name Buffalo Regency used as applied to certain men; from documents written and printed; I have heard of Nazarite Band and Nazarite Union, both of which terms, as I understand, implying the same organization. I have never seen in the *Advocate* any notice of any meeting of the Regency, to my knowledge.

Cross Examination.—I first heard the term, Buffalo Regency, used on the Conference floor, at Olean, by Rev. L. Stiles, Jr.; I first saw the name, Nazarite Band, in several documents that providentially fell into my hands; one of these documents contained a plan of organization; the others referred to such form of organization, and to its action in several cases; one of them contained its form of obligation; the commencement of the form of obligation, as nearly as I recollect, is as follows: "In the name of God! Amen. We hereby solemnly vow, &c." This Nazarite Band was a secret society, according to the documents referred to. There was a statement as to the number that belonged to the Union; there were said to be 45 to 50; there were officers, according to the document referred to, Chief Scribe, Scribe and Counsellors. Each man joining had a fictitious name, according to one of the documents; the documents declared that Bro. B. T. Roberts was an officer in said society; Bro. McCreary was the Chief Scribe, known as Bani. Bro. McCreary's name was signed to these documents; I saw these documents about the first of July, 1855.

Rev. JOSEPH McCREARY called.—I wrote two letters to Bro. Wentworth, which were delivered up and read at the Olean Conference; also, two letters to Bro. Gilbert De La Matyr, which were likewise delivered up and read at the Olean Conference; also, one to Joseph Latham. I wrote these letters alone; I wrote everything relating to the Nazarite Band; I wrote the documents; I did design an association, and prepared the documents in anticipation of such; but when we got to Conference we had enough to do of other business. We did not organize, and the question of organization has been an open question ever since; I never administered the vow to any one, and I never took it myself—not formally; cannot say what others may have done; it was proposed in anticipation only; the association never was practically formed; I stated nearly so on the floor of the Olean Conference; I stated that the thing was provisional and prospective, and *I alone was responsible for the whole concern.* As near as I can recollect that was what I said, when called in question for the thing.

Cross Examination.—If I recollect right, I seconded the resolution passed at the Olean Conference, with a loud voice, and voted for it, more out of courtesy to the

Conference than anything else. The Conference seemed determined to pass some kind of a compromise, and I thought that was as harmless as anything else that could be passed, and so I voted for it. I talked about the formation of this band wherever I happened to be with preachers, frequently consulting with two, three, four or five, as we happened to meet together; I can't recollect distinctly when or where we had the first consultation; we never had any formal consultations on the subject. I attended the Genesee district camp meeting at Bergen, 1855; I have no recollection that this subject was talked over there; I do not recollect whether I wrote to Bro. De La Matyr, or whether he was duly elected a member or not—his letter will show. I nominated and appointed a great many members, and notified them thereof; I understood the appointments to be provisional, and the whole concern a fiction—prepared and ready to become a fact, when we should see fit to make it such. I do not recollect writing any letters, saying that persons were elected members; I cannot affirm nor deny it; it sounds just like me. I have seen hundreds of the documents called Documents of the Nazarite Union; I wrote the whole pamphlet, preface and all. I think the number of the preachers with whom, at various times, I spoke on the subject, was about twelve. They thought it would be a nice thing to form such a Union; it struck their fancies; but when the time came to form the Union, they all backed out. The preface to the pamphlet is a mythical concern altogether.

Rev. J. P. KENT called.—I have no knowledge of the existence of any such organization or society as the Nazarite Band or Union. I have been considered as belonging to that class designated as Nazarites; I have always affirmed that I had no knowledge of such a society, and that I believed there was no such society. At the last Conference, I signed a paper with a number of other brethren—which paper I now hold in my hand—printed now for the purpose of disabusing the minds of my brethren, and the public generally. The following is the paper:

GENESEE CONFERENCE MATTERS.

READ AND THEN JUDGE.

Certain reports having been put into circulation, charging a portion of the Ministers of the Genesee Conference of the Methodist Episcopal Church, with the disreputable and unworthy act of having organized a society "bearing certain marks of secrecy," under the name of the "Nazarite Band or Union," the object of which, it has been reported, is to control the appointments, and direct the affairs of the Conference: and this charge implicating many of our Ministers as taking steps unworthy the Christian, and derogatory to the Ministerial character:

Therefore, We the undersigned Members of the Genesee Conference hereby declare, that after careful inquiry, we are fully convinced that no such society has ever existed in the bounds of this Conference. The whole excitement with reference to the supposed organization, grew out of certain letters, indicating the existence of such a society, written by a single individual, who, on the floor of the Olean Conference in 1855, publicly declared, that he alone was responsible for the whole affair. These letters were written without our knowledge, and have never received our approval. Though the existence of such a society has been repeatedly denied in various ways and on numerous occasions, yet in public and in private, and especially through the columns of the Buffalo *Christian Advocate*, these reports have been spread abroad, to the injury of the Ministerial reputation, and Christian influence and usefuluess of numbers of our Ministers, by creating an unjust prejudice against them; among whom are some of our most able and efficient men.

Connected with the charge of association, is that of encouraging fanaticism, and extravagance in Religious exercise and worship. This charge we declare to be as groundless as the other. We have never encouraged excesses, and with them we have not the *least* sympathy. But while we stand opposed to all improprieties in Religious exercises and worship, we declare ourselves in favor of a *consistent* and *vitalized* religion : not a dead formalism, but the power of Godliness. Not that form of Religion that expresses itself in confused irregularities on the one hand, or on the other, in sermons without life and without adaptation,—the abandonment of social meetings, and the neglect of family and private prayer; but in a Religion that moves the heart, and prompts to every good work; not of benificence alone, but also of devotion.

These charges then of forming an association or encouraging fanaticism, having their origin, in the opinion of some, in ambition and jealousy; made and reiterated, it has been feared, with a design and for effect—*if applied to us*, we unhesitatingly pronounce to be unjust, iniquitous, *slanderous* and FALSE.

A. ABELL,	ISAAC C. KINGSLEY,
JOHN P. KENT,	C. D. BURLINGHAM,
SAMUEL C. CHURCH,	A. HARD,
LORREN STILES, Jr.,	B. T. ROBERTS,
JOHN B. JENKINS,	E. S. FURMAN,
W. GORDON,	R. E. THOMAS,
A. W. LUCE,	DANIEL B. LAWTON,
J. MILLER,	WM. KELLOGG,
Le Roy, September, 1857.	J. BOWMAN.

Cross Examination.—I have attended secret, or rather, private meetings, with the persons with whom I have been associated; I never attended a meeting for consultation about the formation of a Nazarite Band or Union; I never attended but two private meetings in my life; I think I was not at one at Le Roy the Tuesday evening before Conference; I was not notified to be at any such meeting. At one of these meetings the subject, and only subject, as far as I recollect was, that who we would elect delegates to the General Conference; I do not recollect what the other was for, but think the subject of signing petitions was talked of. In neither of these meetings nothing was done affecting individual character.

PLEA OF REV. L. STILES.

MR. CHAIRMAN: Indisposed as I find myself at this time by reason of a severe cold, and hence disqualified as I feel myself to speak on this occasion, it is exceedingly fortunate for Bro. Roberts that such is the nature of the case before us, soon to be submitted to the action of this Conference, that he needs but little of my help. Could we all be disposessed of prejudice, arrising from the unfortunate condition into which we are plunged by reason of the party issues that now so unhappily divide us; could we be turned back in the history of our Conference but a few brief years; could we see as we then saw, feel as we then felt, and act as we then acted, we should be now ready, with the testimony before us as we now have it, notwithstanding the lengthy speech of the Council for the prosecution, in which he has twice gone over the whole ground of the matters of complaint, to submit the case to the action of the Conference without a single word of defence on our part. In so doing there could not be a single doubt as to the result. In the unprejudiced judgment of this Conference Bro. Roberts would be immediately, fully and justly, acquitted of the charge alleged against him.

I confess myself not a little surprised that a charge of this character should be brought against the defendant; that anything of this kind should be introduced to further distract and divide our Conference. True, I had heard months ago repeated expressions of a predetermination to expel several of the leading members of this body. It has been iterated and reiterated through the Conference that this thing *must* and *would* be done at this Conference, and that Bro. Roberts was one of the number thus preordained to be expelled. But such seemed to me to be the madness of this enterprise, that I could not believe it would be entered upon. But it seems we have misjudged either the heads or the hearts of these men. And now, as we are put upon our defence under these circumstances, we wish it distinctly understood that as our case is not one that calls for the exercise of mercy, we ask none at the hands of the Conference. If worthy of death we refuse not to die. It was said by the Council of the prosecution in his opening plea with reference to the action of this Conference in the case of Bro. Roberts last year, that "he was allowed to remain in the Conference by the exercise of the extreme of mercy." This we positively deny. He asked no mercy last year, he only asked for justice, which was not granted; and all he asks at this time is simply justice, which if granted will result in his full acquittal.

We fully accord with the sentiment expressed by the counsel for the prosecution, that "important interests are pending upon the issues of this trial; that they will materially effect the people, and the harmony of our Zion." This is unquestionably true, and doubtless, in a far greater degree than we now apprehend! Such is the nature of this prosecution, and the influences which have induced it, that let it result either in acquittal or condemnation, it will most certainly "affect the people and the harmony of our Zion." It is well for us to keep this in mind. The people understand these matters; they will see, and judge, and act in reference to them. We must remember that this case is to go before the tribunal of the people, after it is passed upon by this Conference.

We now come to remark directly upon the charge, specifications and items. The charge is: "*Unchristian, immoral conduct.*" A very grave charge, indeed! Of the highest grade known in our ecclesiastical courts. This fact constituted the basis of our exception to the prosecution of this charge. There is evidently a *design* in the manner in which this bill is framed. The defence is charged with "immoral conduct;" the highest grade of crime known in our ecclesiastical courts. Had he been guilty of theft, adultery, or murder, the charge would have been the same. But the specifications, if proved to be true, look to offences of a very different grade, bearing no likeness as to moral turpitude to the grade mentioned in the charge. This method of proceeding is most unjust, and calculated to reflect unfairly and unjustly upon the defence, whether acquitted or condemned. Last year the same method was adopted to prejudice and damage the character of the defendant. He was pronounced guilty of *immoral conduct,* for the *crime* of writing and publishing an article, all of which he offered to prove true, but was barred of the privilege. And then he was heralded through the land, through the columns of the Buffalo *Advocate,* as guilty of "immoral conduct." None can be in doubt as to the *design* in framing this bill thus.

The first specification under this grave charge is "contumacy," in disregarding the admonition of this Conference in its decision upon his case at its last session.

We have good reason to believe that the defendant did not regard himself as acting contumaciously in the action objected to by the prosecution. He did not, and others did not, understand the vote of the Conference of last year to require him to pursue a course different from what he has taken, or, as the wording of the Minutes seems to have it, "pursue a better course in the future." Or, if contumacy be, as defined by the prosecuting counsel, "stubbornness, with reference to submission to proper order or authority," it is yet to be shown that defendant has manifested such stubbornness; and it is yet to be shown that he has not "pursued a better course." But, suppose it to be granted that he was contumacious in refusing to submit to the admonition of the Conference, is this "immoral conduct?" Is this a crime of the highest grade known in the calendar of crimes? Can we in justice vote this brother guilty of "immoral conduct," for the offence alleged in this specification? Most certainly we cannot do this, and be guiltless ourselves.

SECOND SPECIFICATION.— "In republishing, or assisting in the republication and circulation of, a document entitled "New-school Methodism," the original publication of which had been pronounced by this Conference, unchristian and immoral conduct."

As we understand it, both the publication and circulation must be proved, to sustain the specification. Nothing is made out, unless both are proved. Suppose it were proved that defendant published any given number of said documents, and it could not be proved that any number of them ever went into circulation; or suppose it to be proved that none of them were ever circulated, what culpability could attach to the mere act of publication? Now, as defendant is charged with both publication *and* circulation, both must be proved, or the case fails. But both are not proved; so far from this, we have proved most positively, that Bro. Roberts had nothing whatever to do with the publication of the Estes pamphlet, or the republication of his article of last year. The author of said publications has here testified that he alone was responsible for said publications; that Mr. Roberts never, in any way, to his knowledge, contributed a single cent for the publishing of said articles. We have evidence that Mr. Roberts did not even know of the intention to publish said articles. Thus, we see, while the charge in the one limb of this specification proves groundless, the other goes by default.

Then, too, the evidence as to circulation is quite inadequate to substantiate the specification. It rests alone on the testimony of one man; and the conversation alleged to be had with reference to them was in the cars, under circumstances not the most favorable to ascertaining the truth in the case. He testifies that defendant put three dozen of these fly-sheets into his hands, and requested him to hand them to one or two other persons. Suppose we admit this to be true, and that it is precisely as he states it to be, still it is not yet proved that a single copy of these thirty-six ever went into circulation, except such as were circulated by said witness. No evidence appears whatever, that at any other time, or under any other circumstances, defendant ever circulated a single copy of the fly-sheets. A local preacher, on his charge of the past year, with whom he has been very intimate, testifies that he never saw one of said sheets, till he was on his way to this Conference, which is proof presumptive that he did not circulate them, or he would have been quite likely to have conveyed one to the hands of this intimate friend and local preacher.

Let it be distinctly marked, then, that all the evidence of circulation that has been adduced in the course of this long investigation, rests upon the evidence of this one single witness, under the circumstances above named.

Let it be marked, also, that whatever of criminality there may be in the act of circulating, many others are in the same condemnation, and equally guilty, if not more so. While the prosecution has failed to prove that a single copy ever went into circulation by the agency of Bro. Roberts, we have proved positively that others, who are in opposition to Bro. Roberts, have purchased and circulated numbers of them. Bro. Hopkins has testified that he has purchased two dozen of them, and that, too, we suppose, for the express purpose of circulation. Probably, half or more of the members of this Conference are guilty of the very thing alleged against Bro. Roberts in this specification. This being the case, we would ask, Why this distinction? Why seize upon one man out of seventy-five, or more, who are equally guilty? Why make him the scape-goat to bear away the crimes of a whole Conference?

The answer is, it has been predetermined that this one man must go out of the Conference; and, while all others who are equally guilty are held as guiltless, he must be seized upon as the Conference victim. Then, we ask again, is Bro. Roberts guilty of "immoral conduct?" If so, then we have seventy-five others, all members of this Conference, guilty of "immoral conduct!" A strange state of affairs, indeed! Half of the Genesee Conference guilty of "immoral conduct;"—charges, however, for the very same offense, presented against only *one* of this number!

THIRD SPECIFICATION.—"In publishing, or assisting in the publication and circulation of a document printed in Brockport, and signed Geo. W. Estes, and appended to the one entitled New-school Methodism, and containing, among other libels upon this Conference generally, and upon some of its members particularly, the following, to wit:"

Under this specification we find a bill of items, of things written in the Estes pamphlet, which Bro. Roberts is charged with circulating and publishing, or assisting in so doing. The proof is yet wanting.

This specification charges libel upon the defendant in saying things included in this bill of items.

Before entering upon the investigation of these items, we wish to repudiate the false assumption of the prosecuting counsel, that we endorse, as a whole, the assertions of these items, or the document from which they are taken; or that we do, by any inference or implication, acknowledge the authorship, or confess to the charge of publication or circulation, simply because we enter upon our defense in a legal and legitimate way. By what strange reasoning does the counsel leap to such a forced conclusion as this? Whoever heard of its parallel in any civil or ecclesiastical court before this day? This is a mere assumption of the counsel, utterly without foundation, warrant, or justification; a subterfuge, as we shall see, to *serve an end, and to compass a purpose.**

Here we wish to say distinctly that we do not now and never have endorsed *all* the sentiments of the Estes pamphlet, from which these items are taken. Bro. Roberts does not endorse, in the literal sense, *all* that is said in these items. When I received that proof-sheet, I read it till I came to paragraphs which I did not believe to be literally true, sentiments which I thought better never be uttered, reflections upon the Bishops which I believe unjust; and, hence, I put said proof-sheet within the envelope, and refused to read it through. But there *are* sentiments uttered in these items, which we believe to be both strictly true and important, and our object in entering upon a defense of these truths will be most apparent before we conclude our remarks.

The first item says: "For several years past, there has been the annual sacrifice of a human victim, at the Conference."

To know whether the declaration of this item is true, we should understand what was in the mind of the author. What is to be understood by the term "*Sacrificed?*" No one believes this declaration true in a strictly literal sense. We do not, of course, suppose the author of this pamphlet meant to say that a "human victim" was literally annually immolated and beheaded. The absurdity of such an idea is only equalled by the view taken of this expression by the prosecution. They seem to have nothing else in mind but a *money* sacrifice. *Money, money,* seems to be the commodity of paramount importance, in their eyes. Several hours have been spent by them in the examination of witnesses, to prove that men have not been sacrificed in a money point of

---

* According to this reasoning the defendant must confess to the criminality of the charge, or the court must presume him to be guilty by reason of his presuming to enter upon his defence. This is very like the test of ancient witchcraft, where the suspected subject was proved to be guilty, if he presumed to make for the shore when thrown into the water.

The prosecution were obliged to assume this ridiculous position, from the fact of having utterly failed, as all must see, to either fix the authorship of the pamphlet in question upon the defendant, or to prove that he has aided in the publication or circulation of the same. It is important to keep in mind this ridiculous position of the prosecution, from the fact that upon this most senseless subterfuge, the defendant was finally condemned and expelled from the Conference and the Church, on the charge of "unchristian and immoral conduct!!"

Either this must be confessed, or else an attitude equally uncomplimentary to the head or heart of the prosecution, and one not less farcical and sham like, is forced upon them, viz: That of convicting the defendant of "unchristian and immoral conduct," and of expelling him from the Conference and the M. E. Church, for the act (if such testimony as was presented were allowed to be valid) of putting a three dozen package of the fly sheets into the hands of a neighboring preacher, with the request that he hand them to the third person. And this, too, when perhaps one half of the members of the Conference were equally guilty!!

view. It is concluded that one man who was deemed sacrificed, in the sense of the author of the sheet, was not sacrificed, because, forsooth, it is proved that his salary at the time under question, was a "thousand dollars a year, and his house-rent." Character, reputation, ministerial standing, and Christian influence are all left out of the question by the prosecution! These are of no account; they are passed by unnoticed. The only question of importance to them seems to be, "Did you sustain a loss of dollars and cents?

Now, we hold that this is a very mean, low view of the question—a view, probably, which never entered the mind of the author of this item, and would only be entertained by a lover of mammon. If, for adherence to the truth, I were turned out to beg from door to door, or to saw wood for my daily bread, I would scorn the idea of talking about being sacrificed, in a mere money point of view. In the sense designed by the author of the item, we have proved conclusively that men have been sacrificed. In a very important sense, the ministerial reputation and standing, and the Christian influence of certain men in this Conference, have been sacrificed by a secret combination of certain other men in this Conference, instituted to crush them out, and drive them from the Conference. Here, then, in this item, is no libel, for what is said is strictly true, in the sense doubtless designed by its author.

Are we then prepared, as a Conference, to vote a man guilty of "Immoral, unchristian conduct," for the act of circulating such a truth as this? Who dare raise his hand to pronounce the act "immoral conduct?"

The second item of this specification, importing libel to the defendant, is the following, viz., "No man is safe, who dares even whisper a word against this secret Inquisition in our midst."

Here, again, we have to remark that the sense of the author of the item should be sought for.

Much time has been spent by the prosecution, in the examination of witnesses, to prove that there is not really a literal "Inquisition" in our Conference. Well, who ever dreamed there was? Who ever supposed we had the literal thing among us? None of us have ever supposed that in any dark corner of our Conference, we had, under bar and bolt, enclosed by walls, the literal dungeon, fire, fagot, rack, thumbscrews and gridirons. Nothing of this kind was in the mind of the author. But that there is something in our midst that bears a strong and sharp likeness, image, and superscription to the spirit of the Inquisition, who will presume to deny, after all we have seen in the progress of this trial? When we see what we have here—a P. E. going around with his little common-place book, picking up the little confidential whisperings, uttered in social chit-chat, and bringing them up to this Conference, and presenting them as bars to the admission of a young man to our Conference—who, we say, in view of this and many other things of a like nature we have been called to witness, will say the author was not justifiable in the utterance of the sentiment of the item? Who, indeed, will feel himself safe hereafter in "whispering a word against this secret Inquisition?" Who, in looking at what we believe to be the meaning of this item, can vote B. T. Roberts guilty of "unchristian and immoral conduct," from the proof adduced of circulating this pamphlet? This can not be done in righteousness or in Justice.

The third item is that with reference to "bankruptcies and adulteries," being "venal offences" in the eyes of these men of the "secret Inquisition."

As we have already announced that we did not endorse all the language of all these items, and have not designed to attempt to prove or justify each and every sentence

3

and sentiment contained therein, we will remark only upon that clause upon which testimony has been brought to bear.

As to the charge of bankruptcy, the case upon which testimony has been adduced, we regard as proof sufficient to show that there was, at least, some very plausible grounds upon which to base the assertion, and justify the charge. True, a certificate has been produced, showing that a disciplinary investigation was had in the case; but we have evidence to show that at least three of the injured creditors knew nothing about said investigation; that, although two of them were prominent citizens of the village of Lima, where the investigation was had, these men were wholly ignorant of its occurrence. Here is a strange feature in the case! Does it not, we would ask, at least look in the direction of *fraudulent* bankruptcy? Then, too, the unwillingness that has been shown by members of this Conference to have this matter looked into, is, to say the least, a very shabby compliment to the integrity and intentions of the parties concerned. As will be remembered, letters were presented at the Medina Conference, purporting to convey important information, concerning the character of the bankruptcy of Rev. Wm. H. De P. These letters were from the hands of injured parties, who desired redress, if redress could be had. The request was made that these letters be referred to a committee, that should be appointed by the Conference, to examine their contents, with the express understanding, that if the grounds of complaint which they set forth were unworthy of Conference action, that they be permitted to slumber in the hands of the committee. But, strange to say, this impartial effort to secure an honorable investigation of this bankruptcy was treated with neglect, the committee was refused, and the matter passed by in comparative silence. With these facts before us, we are quite willing to leave every unpredudiced mind to find how much and how good grounds there are for the charge of the item under consideration.

Item fourth says: "The same fifty men who voted Bro. Roberts guilty of "unchristian and immoral conduct," for writing the above article, voted to re-admit a brother from the regions round about Buffalo, for the service performed of kissing a young lady, in the vestibule of the Conference room, during the progress of Bro. Robert's trial. "Nero fiddled while the martyrs burned."

About all we have to say with reference to this item is, we suppose it to be highly figurative, and from respect to the feeling of the person implicated as having kissed the girl, for the consideration named in this item, we pass it by with but few remarks. Whether admission to this Conference was really the *bona fide* consideration for the service performed, I have no special means of knowing, and, hence, have no disposition to making any further remarks on the subject.

The fifth item reads thus: "Bro. Robert's trial, if it deserves the name of a trial, was marked by gross iniquity of proceedings."

The grounds of this charge we suppose to be based, not so much upon the mere acts of the trial, in the court-room, as upon the outside connections of the trial, in their bearings on the actions in the court-room.

To avoid the force of the truth of this item, the prosecuting counsel has gravely told us that, "We have nothing to do with what took place out of the court room. We have only to do with the actual acts of the trial."* Could this position be granted, it would certainly be a very cheap way of disposing of, to the prosecution, a very unpleasant difficulty. But we doubt not that every unbiased mind will decide

---

* See note on page 32.

that outside influences have very much to do with the integrity of the acts in the court room. Suppose an empanneled jury, prior to taking their places in the jury box, to enter a private room, and by themselves alone there discuss in any way the merits of an important criminal case, soon to be brought before them for decision. Suppose them there to take *test* votes bearing upon the case, and then to express in any way their opinions relative to the guilt or innocence of the criminal. What, we would ask, would be said of such jurymen? We all know that the world would justly brand them with infamy. They would well deserve the contempt and scorn of every honest man, and would go out to the world marked with perfidy, dark as that which stained the Harden County Jury. But what less than this criminality do we see in the action pertaining to the trial of Rev. R. T. Roberts at the Le Roy Conference? Mark the parallel! Here we see a body of Methodist Ministers who are to act as jurors in the trial of a brother preacher, going by themselves into a private room, holding a secret meeting, to all intents and purposes, pledging themselves together to "*keep to themselves the proceedings of the meeting.*" Then after discussion had in the case, taking *test* votes bearing upon the case, and after pledging to proceed against Bro. Roberts, then we see them coming into the court room and acting in perfect accordance with the votes taken in the secret meeting. Now when we look at what we here see, these men acting in a sacredly pledged secret meeting, held in a private room over Bryant and Clark's store in Le Roy, there prejudging and pre-enacting in the case of Bro. Roberts, and then coming into the court room in the M. E. Church and acting as they did then and there act, with such perfect unanimity that in voting on the specifications and the charge, there was hardly the variation among them of a hand, more or less, that went up on each and every specification and the charge. When we connect, we say, the transactions of these two rooms and these two meetings, and compare the harmony of action in both cases, we would ask how dissimilar are these transactions to those of the perjured jurors, to whom reference has been made for illustration? And we would ask with how good a grace does the prosecuting counsel say, "We have nothing to do with what took place out of the court room." And again we would ask, and claim an answer at the lips of every honest man, was not "Bro. Roberts' trial marked by gross iniquity of proceedings?" And for saying this, in view of the circumstances we have brought to view in the case, should any one be charged with either unchristian or immoral conduct? Most certainly not.

The sixth and seventh items are withdrawn, for reasons we suppose well understood by the prosecution.

The eighth item says of a certain "venerable D. D.," that "Though nominally superannuated, &c., he is nevertheless quite efficient in embarrassing effective preachers in their work and pleading them to hell for the crime of preaching and writing the truth." I suppose the author of this item fixed his mind upon facts which have transpired in this Conference, and then said just what he believed to be true.

It is a well known fact that this "venerable D. D." has been quite efficient in embarrassing effective preachers in their work."

Three successive Conferences at least, preceding the present, have borne witness to the fact that this "venerable D. D." has been chief agent in bringing "Bills of Information" and "Bills of Charges" against effective preachers, and as this author says, so doubtless he believed, for "preaching and writing the truth." Certainly it can be no small embarrassment in the way of the effective men of the Conference, to have an annual Bill of Charges brought against them by this venerable D. D., whatever may be the result of the investigation; and certainly these men against whom charges have been brought, have been "effective men," men whose labors have been greatly blessed of the Lord; men whose labors have year after year been followed by extensive revivals of religion; and "that this "venerable D. D." did plead Bro. Roberts to hell" at the Le Roy Conference in the paper he read on the Conference floor, will not be doubted by any who remember the import of that remarkable document.

The ninth item reads thus: "There is a clique among us called the "Buffalo Regency," conspiring and acting in secret conclave to kidnap or drive away, or proscribe and destroy by sham trials and starvation appointments, every one who has the boldness to question their supremacy in the Conference."

That there is a "clique among us called the Buffalo Regency," none I think will ever hereafter be able to deny.

It seems myself had the honor of publicly christening this secret clique. I was not aware that in a little speech on the Olean Conference floor I was doing so notable an act. I had frequently heard this name given to this clique on various occasions, but never dreamed that I was to have the distinguished honor of first pronouncing in public the name of "Buffalo Regency."

I concede however that it is clearly proven; for the prosecution have called on witness after witness to prove that they first heard the name spoken by myself on the floor of the Olean Conference.

We will here rest the important question as to the public baptism of this secret clique called the Buffalo Regency. The name is conceded. Now, that we have the veritable thing for the design specified in the item, we have clearly shown by many witnesses.

The efforts made by the prosecution to prove there is not an actual organization claiming this name, are all utterly void of force and importance. We have never believed and never asserted that this clique had an actual constitution and by-laws, and that in due form they held their annual election for officers, and were surrounded by all the paraphernalia of a regularly organized secret society, as in the case of the Odd Fellows or Masons. But what we contend for, and what we have proved, is that this clique actually do act as a secret society. And while they have not the constitution and by-laws, they have the veritable thing.

We have shown that this clique have held regular secret meetings; as strictly secret and private as any meetings ever known as secret meetings.

We have shown that at one of those meetings, at least, a door-keeper was employed to guard the room and prevent the entrance of all who could not be trusted. And it is a notable fact that this witness in his unwillingness to tell the facts in the case, has testified to the strange circumstance that he "*Stood outside of all the Churches in Medina.*" This testimony, strange as it is, is not without its significancy, which we shall do well to remember.

So secret were those meetings that even a brother preacher from a neighboring Conference could not be trusted. And after due private deliberation as to how to get rid of the unwelcome guest, a member of the secret clique went to said brother and duly informed him that that was a secret meeting and he was invited to leave the room. There was, as we have shown, not only a general understanding among the members of this clique, that these meetings were to be secret, but we see them taking the precaution, lest in some way these proceedings should leak out, to "pledge themselves to keep to themselves the proceedings of the meeting." No further proof, then, is necessary, that this Regency Clique is a *secret* clique.

In the extreme desire of the prosecution to avoid the culpability consequent upon the proof adduced of the nature of these secret meetings, they have resorted to a characteristic dodge which reminds us very forcibly of an adage of Dr. Bond, viz : "*He that is only law honest is a very great rogue.*"

Witnesses have here been asked, "If they were in any *secret* meetings held in Le Roy during the session of our Conference there? They have answered in the negative. When other facts were to be elicited, these witnesses have been asked, "Were you in a *select* meeting held over Bryant and Clark's store in Le Roy, during the session of our Conference there, and they have answered in the affirmative. Is it not passing strange that Methodist Ministers should stoop so low as to resort to such trickery and deception as this to avoid the force of truth? These men have solemnly testified here, with all due gravity, that they positively were not in any *secret* meetings, but that they were in *select* meetings at the time under consideration, and we have adduced evidence to show that these meetings bore all the essential characteristics and attributes of strictly secret meetings. Yet they were not *secret*, only *select* meetings! Here surely is a distinction without a difference. After the close of the Le Roy Conference, on my way to the depot, I exchanged a few words with a brother on the subject of the secret meetings, which I supposed had been held during the session of our Conference. To my utter astonishment this brother positively denied that the Regency men had had a single *secret* meeting during the session of that Conference. Not an hour after that, before I had passed ten miles from Buffalo, a brother minister told me in the cars that he had during the session of our Conference been in a *secret* meeting of those men. This brother when invited in was supposed to be in sympathy with them. As I supposed both of these brethren to be men of unquestionable veracity, I was wholly unable to reconcile these antagonistic statements. But during the progress of this trial the mystery is all solved. These were not *secret*, but only *select* meetings.

The business transactions of these meetings, present, according to the testimony of those who were in there, a strange mongrel of the social and religious aspect. Evidence goes to show that the business of these meetings was transacted in a business like manner. There was the Chairman who presided over their deliberations, and there was the Secretary who kept a record of the proceedings of the meeting. We have exhibited before this Conference the minutes of one of these meetings, which shows that motions were duly made, put, passed and recorded. Evidence shows that as to the business of these meetings, there was passing upon the character of preachers, praying, eating peaches, talking upon the subject of holiness, discussion of disciplinary questions, signing petitions or remonstrances against preachers who were obnoxious to them, &c., &c.

All this was done, you will observe, in a business like and very pious manner. True, those of us who are uninitiated, cannot comprehend fully why a Chairman and Secretary should be necessary in a meeting for talking on the subject of holiness, or of prayers, or why these meetings should be held within closed doors, or why minutes of the same should be kept, or why a brother minister should be invited out of a meeting held for so a good a purpose, or why a door keeper should be necessary; and yet such is the evidence in the case.

The proof then, of the assertion of this item, that these men did " act in secret conclave," is past all doubt. That a part of their business was to take measures to "drive away" those who had the "boldness to question their supremacy in Conference," I think is quite as evident; and that this "driving away process," was to be pursued in part, at least, by "sham trials," is most evident, as evinced especially in the trial of Bro. Roberts of last year.

We are fully justified in calling the proceedings of these trials "sham trials." First, from the fact that these trials are prejudged and predetermined, as our evidence shows. It has been understood for months past that this trial was to take place at this Conference. Expressions to this effect have here and there leaked out and come to our ears. It has been said that these men, who are opposed to this secret clique that we have so fully exposed, *must* and *would* be put out of the Conference at this session, and Bro. Roberts has been named as one of the persons who *must* be thus sacrificed according to the predetermination and dictation of this secret clique.

One of these leading men of this secret clique said, prior to Bro. Roberts' trial last year, " *Those men must be sacrificed and they will be ; I know the minds of the leading men in this Conference on this point, and also of the Bishops.*"

In justice to our bench of Bishops I here take pleasure in saying that these reflections upon their integrity we brand as grossly unjust and calumnious. We do not now, and we never have believed that these men ever had any good reason to say that they "knew the minds of the Bishops on this subject." We never have believed that the Bishops ever designed to show any party partiality towards either of the party sections of our Conference. If we had no other evidence of the impartiality of the Bishops in our Conference issues, I think that the total absence of the slightest appearance of favoritism during the progress of this perplexing and laborious trial, should be sufficient to disabuse any candid mind of so unfounded a suspicion. And yet this talk is no new thing to us. This is not the first time that we have heard from the same quarters, by the same class of men, that the Bishops were committed to the favor of the Regency party, and against the Nazarites. These things have been stated to the laity for party purposes and to serve personal ends. We regard, as we always have, these declarations as unjust in their reflections upon the Bishops, as they are void of truth. We repudiate such statements as slanders upon the Episcopacy, which as far as they are believed, are calculated to do them great injustice.

But to return to the culpability on the part of the prosecution of prejudging and predetermining this case : Bro. Roberts was named by this man, who made the remark we have quoted, as one of the men who "must be sacrificed." One of these leading men said in a private family only a few miles distant from this place, on his way to this Conference, "some of these men must be put out of the Conference at this session, and we have the *tools* to do it with."

In yonder Chapel but a few hours since it was said by one of these secret clique men, "one of these parties must be driven to the wall at this Conference." Witnesses have testified that men of that secret clique party have told them during the year, that two or three of the leading men of the so called Nazarite party were to be expelled at this Conference.

To break the force of our witness on this point as to "sham trials," the prosecution has asked a witness "If one of these expressions was not uttered during a conversation on the evils of Nazaritism." Here again we find the "dog Noble" barking away at the empty hole of Nazaritism, where he has been barking for the past three years. We have shown that there is not the slightest evidence that any such a society ever existed. Bro. G. McCreary has here testified, and as he did also three years ago at the Olean Conference, that he alone was responsible for whatever had been written, indicating that such a society ever existed. Such has been the understanding ever since, and yet the empty hole is again assailed by the barking dog Noble. From the fact of the persistent determination of these men to insist upon the existence of a Nazarite society, a few of us who considered ourselves misrepresented at the Le Roy Conference, published a disclosure, setting this matter in its true light, which you will find in the testimony of Rev. J. P. Kent.

But, suppose we admit that these remarks were made during a conversation on "the evils of Nazaritism," what then ?

We deny positively, that any such evils exist among those who are called Nazarites, as are charged upon them. We know positively that the charges of excesses and extravagances in religious devotions, imputed to them, are absolutely and grossly false and slanderous, and that they have not the slightest foundation in truth ; and we doubt not these reflections upon them are made for party purpose and effect. Talk about the *evils* of Nazaritism ! Sir, the time has come among us, when evil is put for good, and good for evil ; bitter for sweet, and sweet for bitter ; light for darkness, and darkness for light.

This question was asked a witness : " Was not the opinion based on the fact, if they continued to pursue this irregular course, they were to be put out of Conference ?" What palliation of the iniquity of prejudging these men, and predetermining to expel them from the Conference, is this, we would wish to know, even if this should prove to be true, which was not so proved. This only shows that these men assume to say what is regular, and what is irregular. It has come to that, that a few men assume to be the self-constituted regulators of the Conference ; but it so happens that we question their claims in this matter. What they call regular, in some matters, we call very irregular ; and what they call irregular, we call regular. This Conference has been so long *regulated* by these irregular men, as we hold them, that things are found to be in a very *irregular* condition among us.

We call these trials sham-trials again, from the fact of their having been virtually decided, as we have clearly and fully shown, by the jurors, prior to their coming into the court-room. We will not detain the Conference, to detail these revolting circumstances again. These test-votes, and these secret pre-enactments, are before you. The attempt, by the prosecution, to avoid the inevitable rebuke and condemnation that must fall upon the perpetrators of these deeds of secret injustice, which we have brought to light by prying open the doors of the secret conclaves, by saying that they "voted that the character of B. T. Roberts should not pass till he had a *fair trial,*" is another baseless artifice, that all unprejudiced minds will look upon in in its true light. We have already seen what these men call " a fair trial." What they call " fair," we pronounce most unjust and unfair ; and we believe that the unprejudiced judgment of the church and the community will pronounce such secret-meeting proceedings as were had in Bro. Roberts' case of last year, not only unjust and unfair, but will brand such trial proceedings as sham-like and grossly unjust.

The sham nature of these trials is seen, again, in the partiality of the subjects upon whom they are fixed. If it is matter of guilt, or moral wrong, to circulate these flysheets, and if we should acknowledge that this guilt or wrong-doing was proved against Bro. Roberts, and if a penalty of any nature is to be inflicted on him for said acts, then, we wish to know, why fix on one, or two, or three men of this Conference as worthy of charges and Conference censure, while many others in the Conference, equally guilty, are passed by unnoticed ? Why this making the very same act a venal offence in one man, and a mortal sin in another? Why, we ask, is Rev. B. T. Roberts fixed upon as guilty and blame-worthy, when those who stand opposed to him in the matters of our Conference issues, are unnoticed, though guilty of the very same thing charged upon him? Mr. Chairman, we need not ask why; for we know why. It is simply, sir, because he is a man "who has the boldness to question the supremacy, in this Conference," of the clique known as the Buffalo Regency. This seems to be about the head and front of the offending of Bro. Roberts. Did he not "question their supremacy," and damage their craft, and expose their secret plottings, and make bare their wrong-doings, and wrong doctrines and teachings, this bill of charges had never been presented against him, and four days of the time of this Conference would not have been consumed in the traversing of this case. The prosecuting counsel, in a fruitless effort to worm himself out of this dark feature in this palpable injustice perpetrated against Bro. Roberts, says, "What have we to do with others? He is the man. The question is not, Have *others* circulated these documents? but, Has Bro. Roberts circulated them." Exactly so! *This is precisely the question!* The question is not, how many others have circulated them? Or how many of them have others circulated? These are questions of no importance whatever. The all important question is, has Bro. Roberts circulated them? And why we beg to know is this the question? The answer is at hand in the language of this item. It is simply and solely, because he "Has the boldness to question the supremacy in our Conference," of this Buffalo Regency clique. Let this fact be distinctly kept in mind. Did Bro. Roberts pusillanimously submit to the arbitrary dictation and control of this secret clique in our Conference, he would to-day be in as high esteem among these men as any brother in the Conference. But, sir, he has involved himself in difficulty, simply because he has the manliness, integrity and boldness to question the supremacy of, and hurl defiance at a secret power in our Conference, which marks every man as a victim who does not submit to its arbitrary rule.

Having thus reviewed these items in the light of the testimony before us, and having seen the cloud of facts that come in to substantiate the truthfulness of all the points we have attempted to sustain, we are willing to submit to the decision of any impartial tribunal, the question, should Bro. Roberts, or any other man, be pronounced guilty of "unchristian and immoral conduct," for uttering the sentiments of these items. Had the efforts been successful to prove that Bro. Roberts had published and circulated the fly sheet, this Conference could not, with any show of justice, pronounce him guilty of "unchristian and immoral conduct," for publishing those sections in these items, the sentiments of which we have vindicated and shown to be true, in the light of the evidences and facts we have presented to this Conference.

But the efforts of the prosecution to prove the agency of Bro. Roberts in the publication and circulation, have been a palpable failure. We have proved by the publisher of the pamphlet, that Bro. Roberts had not the slightest agency in its publication; that he never contributed in any way a single cent for that object, and it does not appear that Bro. Roberts even knew of the intention of its publication until after it was issued.

There is not, then, as all must see, the slightest ground upon which to base a pretext for the conviction of the defendant; and his conviction under these circumstances would be an outrage on justice, scarce ever paralleled in the history of ecclesiastical jurisprudence.

It will be well for us to remember that whatever may be the action of this Conference in this case, that after we have passed upon it, it is to go before the tribunal of the Church and the world. Whatever may be our decision, their verdict will, doubt-less, be that of acquittal. We should remember that the influences of this trial are not to be confined to this court room. Without doubt, it will "affect the people and the harmony of our Zion." The people are watching with intense interest our action in this case, and it will not answer for us to say, as has been said by the prosecution, "what have we to do with outside influences?" We shall learn that we have much to do "with outside influences," and "outside influences" have much to do with us.

As I love the Church of my choice, in which I have lived and labored for the past few years, and in which I mean to live and labor until I die, so deeply do I feel an interest in the influences of this trial on the harmony and peace of our Methodist Zion in this section of the work. Such are the surrounding influences of this trial, the influences which have induced it and the issues pending, that its results upon the interests of our Church must inevitably be wide spread and lasting for good or evil.

Bro. Roberts is well known to be an ardent lover of, and zealous defender of, the Methodist Episcopal Church. From a special intimacy with him for years past, I know as but few others do, how deep and ardent are his attachments to our Church. I know he loves it as he loves his life, and is willing to suffer and die in its service. His labors in this Church of his choice have been remarkably blessed of the Lord, since he entered its ministry. Wherever he has labored, God has given him seals of his ministry, and favor with the people. The past year has been one of marked success in his ministry. The people expect and desire his return. It is well known that he has so endeared himself to the people of his several charges, as but few among us have ever done. To all appearances, as bright a future of usefulness and of minis-terial success lies before him, if permitted to labor on uninterruptedly, as that of any man in our Conference. Now, can it be possible, with the evidences of the innocency of the defendant which we have before us, that we, as a Conference, shall dare in any way, to peril his career of usefulness, by pronouncing Conference censure upon him, for a single act, even if said act be admitted to have transpired, of which, if he be blameworthy at all, he only stands in equal condemnation with, perhaps, half of the members of this Conference? If from the evidences and the facts in the case we now have before us, Benjamin T. Roberts is worthy of Conference censure in any degree, then, we ask, emphatically, where is the man among us who is guiltless? "Let him who is without sin cast the first stone."

CLOSING PLEA BY REV. B. T. ROBERTS.

MR. PRESIDENT: It is fitting that I should, in this public manner, before this large audience, express to you my sincere thanks for the able and impartial manner in which you have presided during this protracted investigation. Whatever the result may be, I shall always cherish for you, sir, the liveliest feelings of gratitude for the kindness you have manifested to me personally, and the equitable spirit which has prompted the decisions which you have, from time to time, been obliged to make.

Fathers and brethren of the Conference: I will not endeavor to conceal from you the disappointment I felt, in not being able to procure a committee, as provided for in the discipline. But as you have chosen to take the decision of the case into your own hands, I trust you will remember that in reality the same responsibility rests upon you personally, as though the determination of the question devolved upon each one of you alone. For months intimations have been current * that several who have been instrumental in promoting what such veterans of the cross as Rev. John P. Kent and Rev. Asa Abell consider nothing more nor less than the life and power of godliness, must be put out of the Conference. The *Advocate* of last week says: "For years past a disturbing element has existed in it, which the conservative and leading portion of the body are determined to control and put out if possible during the present session." No one can mistake the meaning of this language. Does the editor speak by authority when he says, "the leading portion," the Regency, "ARE DETERMINED to *put out the disturbing element*," the leaders of the opposing party? Will you, by your action, show that the result to be arrived at in this and similar cases, has been "determined" upon long ago, without any regard to the testimony adduced, and the facts elicited? Certain it is that in ordinary times, by unprejudiced men, no notice whatever would be taken of such charges as those against us; much less could an adverse decision be obtained.

In the examination of witnesses, we have gone into the details of this case, not because we deemed it necessary to our complete vindication, but because we would have your eyes open to the state of things that exist among us, as a Conference. The brethren of the other side have repeatedly denied that they have any secret society or any secret meetings. In our charity we believed that there were many honest men in the Conference who, blinded by these protestations, were led to give their countenance to schemes they would never tolerate, if the delusion was dissipated and things made to appear as they are. For their sakes we have opened the secret

---

* The *Advocate* of Aug. 26th, says of Mr. Roberts: "*The truth is, the days of his darling schemes of ambition are nearly numbered.*" This is the tone of one confident that he is, at least, the mouthpiece of those who have the power of life and death; and who have resolved upon their victim! Omnipotence itself could hardly use more positive language!

chambers of iniquity, and permitted you to see men professing godliness—the accredited ministers of Jesus Christ—plotting under the pledge of secrecy, and in the guise of devotion to the Church, the overthrow of their unsuspecting brethren. I shall not go into details; my friend has done that ably and fully. In my remarks I shall confine myself to those points, that have, as I conceive, a direct bearing upon the question at issue. I shall pass over all which, however important in itself, is irrelevant to the case.

This trial grows out of the one of last year. I am charged with "contumacy," in disregarding the action of this Conference at its last session. I do not know in what way I disregarded its action. When friends came in the dead of the night and informed me of the action of the Conference in my case, I arose from my couch, put on my apparel, and repaired with all haste to the Conference room, and received, with resignation, the reproof that the Bishop was directed to administer. If there was any admonition to pursue a better course in the future, I am sure I never heard of it until this present trial was commenced. I was not present when the vote was taken, but I have enquired of several reliable brethren who were, and they think there was no such addition to the reproof. But it so stands upon the Journal, and such we must presume to be the action of the Conference.* But be that as it may, I have honestly endeavored to do better than I have ever done before. I have tried to be instant in season and out of season, always abounding in the work of the Lord. I have gone, "not only to those who wanted me, but to those who wanted me most." The Lord has been pleased to own my unworthy, though sincere efforts, to promote His cause, to a greater degree than in any former period of my ministry. He has permitted me to see many souls rejoice in a present, free and full salvation, who one year ago were walking in the ways of sin and death. I believe in growing in grace; and it appears to me that I have grown in grace the past year; and if spared I will endeavor to in the year to come.

If the want of a cordial acquiescence in the justice of the decision of last year be contumacy, then am I contumacious. I always felt that that trial was a farce, and that decision an outrage. Fifty-two men voted me guilty of "immoral and unchristian conduct," when I knew I was not guilty. Galileo was once compelled by a council that claimed as much wisdom and infallibility as this body of ministers can, to retract his statement that the earth moved instead of the sun. But after his retraction, he was heard to say in an under tone, "but the earth does move after all." Their saying that our planet stands still, did not make it so. Voting a man immoral, does not render him immoral. The vote of last year, obtained as it was, did not occasion me the loss of self respect; nor did it lessen, so far as I could learn, in the slightest degree, the confidence which those who know me have always honored me with. Nor could I ever persuade myself that those who voted me guilty of immorality, in reality believed this to be the case.† I made no retraction nor apology. No effort was put forth to explain away the force of what I had written. I constantly affirmed that I believed it to be true, and I offered to prove it if a fair chance were given me; yet these same men who voted me guilty of immorality, voted to pass my character,

_____

* The Secretary is one of the strongest partisans of the Regency faction in the Conference.

† The man who figures most conspicuously in the prosecutions against Mr. Roberts said last year, after he had put forth the most strenuous exertions to convict him of immorality, "I believe if there is a good man in the Conference that enjoys Religion, it is Bro. Roberts."

and sent me forth to preach the Gospel. I must believe then, *that they voted me guilty when they did not believe this to be the case; or, it is their deliberate judgment, expressed in the most solemn manner, that immorality does not unfit a man for being a Minister of Jesus Christ.*

The article on New School Methodism, which was the ostensible cause of the trial last year; as also of the present one, was written in good faith, and with all the candor and impartiality that I could command. For years the Conference has been divided; different members of the Regency party have from time to time published what we conceived to be very unfair accounts of the question at issue. These representations, usually made in the Buffalo *Advocate*, being uncontradicted, were producing their effects. Many began to think they must be true, or a contrary statement would be made. We thought the time had come for us to set forth our views of the ground of the decision; I wished to do it fairly. If we were holding a discussion with the Universalists, as they have no written common creed, and we should find in their paper an article written by one of their leading men, on the points at issue, and no one dissented from this article, we should be treating them with controversial fairness if we quoted it, and held them as a sect responsible. This is the principle on which controversies are generally conducted; I adopted this plan. I found in " *The Advocate*" of the Buffalo Regency two articles written by the literary champion of the party, on the doctrines which constitute, as I believe, the real issue in this Conference. I waited some six or eight weeks and no one expressed a dissent from the views thus publicly put forth: on the contrary, I heard that the articles were endorsed by leading men of the party. I thought, then, that I should be treating them with greater fairness by giving their views in the language of one of their own writers than in any other way; I quoted a paragraph at the time and showed wherein we differed; the article was submitted to the Rev's. Asa Abell, E. S. Furman and John Bowman; * they thought it a just statement of the differences that agitate this Conference. The article was published over my own proper signature; I have reason to believe that disinterested persons, capable of judging, saw nothing in it morally wrong. A minister occupying, by appointment of the General Conference, a prominent position in the Church, wrote me as follows: " Your article appears to me to be written in as mild and candid a tone as such facts can be stated in." A Presiding Elder and prominent member of one of the Eastern Conferences, an entire stranger to me personally, on seeing my article in the papers, wrote me, thanking me for having written it, saying that the new Divinity was creeping into their Conference, and doing immense mischief, and exhorting me to " keep the monster in the light." A leading member of another Conference said: " On reading your article I was particularly struck with its candor." If I misrepresented any one (as I do not think I did) it was unintentional. The same paper in which my article was published was open for a reply; but none was furnished: they chose to meet me with votes rather than with argument.

Before the trial was commenced, I stated in open Conference, " that I had written the article on New School Methodism in good faith, and with a desire to do justice to all concerned; I had, as I supposed, good reason to hold the party responsible for the views set forth in the articles in the *Advocate*, from which I quoted; if I was mistaken I would be glad to correct the mistake; if the brethren concerned will say that those articles do not represent their views, I will publish in the *Independent* and in all the

---

* The latter was well qualified to judge, having been identified with the Regency party.

other papers that they may desire me to, that I was mistaken, that they do not hold the views which I said they did." What more could I do? If I had misrepresented them, through mistake, I was anxious to do all I could to make amends; if I was laboring under a false impression in regard to their views, were they not bound as men, and as christians, when I sought to be corrected, to make the correction. Yet no one said he had been misrepresented; no disavowal was made of the doctrines that I imputed to them. Can it be wondered at that their silence, under these circumstances, confirmed me in the conviction that what I had written was true? If I was mistaken why not give me the authority to correct it? Does not their course evidence that I was not mistaken? They brought a charge against me of "immoral and unchristian conduct," for writing that article. In the specifications they charge me with writing what I never wrote. It is a well established principle of common law, that in all actions for libel, the precise language complained of as libelous must be set forth in the complaint. It will not do to say, "or words to that effect," or "it amounts to that." There is no safety in any other principle.

Yet I was charged with saying what I never said or intended, and what cannot be made out of my words by any honest construction. Thus the first specification reads: "In publishing in the Northern Independent that there exists in the Genesee Conference an associate body, numbering about thirty, whose teaching is very different from that of the fathers of Methodism." I never published any such thing. I say, "Already there is springing up among us a class of preachers whose teaching is very different from that of the fathers of Methodism. They may be found here and there throughout our Zion; but in the Genesee Conference they act as an associate body. They number about thirty." There is an essential difference between "existing" and "acting" as an associate body. "To exist as an associate body," implies a permanent organization; but men may "act as an associate body," who never saw one another before, and who may never meet again.

Though I never affirmed that they "exist as an associate body," yet I had no doubt of it; I did not say it, yet I offered to prove it.

As the Association is a secret one, its existence could be proved only by some of its members. One of them was called upon the stand. He was questioned about his knowledge of a secret Association, composed of members of this Conference. The question was objected to. It was decided that the question must be framed so as to embody this idea: "Do you know of an associate body of men, numbering about thirty, whose *teaching is very different from that of the fathers of Methodism?*" Thus the witness was called upon to do two things which no court of equity would have required — first, to criminate himself; second, to become a judge of opinion. He should have stated what they taught, and left it for the Court to determine whether it accorded with the doctrines of the fathers of Methodism, or not. Thus restricted, I made no farther attempt to examine witnesses.

The second specification charges me with "publishing, as above, that said members of the Genesee Conference are opposed to what is fundamental in Christianity—to the nature itself of Christianity."

I published nothing like it. This is what I said: "It," (the Conference,) "is divided. . . . This difference is fundamental. It does not relate to things indifferent, but to those of the most vital importance. It involves nothing less than the nature itself of Christianity." Who does not know that parties may differ about "what is fundamental in Christianity," and yet neither of them be opposed to it?

The Calvinists and Armenians differ about the atonement; and yet neither of them are opposed to the atonement. We differ from the Baptists about baptism; and yet neither are opposed to baptism.

Upon the principle they pursued, it would be just as easy to condemn the Saviour as myself. A Jew brings against him the charge of slander, or libel. Specification— "In saying that Moses, Job, and Daniel were thieves and robbers." Proof—In the tenth chapter of John, it is recorded that Jesus said: "ALL THAT EVER CAME BEFORE ME ARE THIEVES AND ROBBERS." This is a broad assertion. He makes no exception nor qualification. It cannot be denied that Moses, Job, and Daniel came before him, therefore he says that Moses, Job, and Daniel are thieves and robbers.

This is better reasoning than that by which I was convicted, last year, of "immoral and unchristian conduct."

The testimony taken in this case shows the manner in which the verdict of last year was obtained. It is proved that "select" meetings were held, over Bryant & Clark's store; that "brethren present" in these "select" meetings, "pledged themselves, by rising, to keep to themselves the proceedings of this meeting." This is what the Minutes say; and De Forest Parsons, who tells us he was Chairman of those meetings, "thinks THEY DID" so pledge themselves. Such proceedings were had in these "select" meetings, that it was not considered safe to allow a stranger, who had been invited in, to remain. THOMAS CARLTON tells us, his "impression is, that some one, not a member of our Conference, was invited to go out. Some one spoke to him, and he went out. Why should he be with us, when we were talking of Conference matters? And some one spoke to him, and he went out!"

Why was this brother invited to go out, if nothing improper was expected to be done? If "talking over Conference matters" was a sufficient reason for excluding him from those "select" meetings, would it not be an equally good reason for excluding strangers from the Conference room? It is evident why they wished him to go out. They intended to do something that would not bear the light. If these meetings were seasons of such "great spiritual interest" as one witness would have us believe, and if they were devoted, as Bro. Carlton has endeavored to convince us, in his examination of witnesses, to *consultations about the best modes of promoting revivals of religion, the work of holiness, and the enforcement of the discipline,* it would seem that this brother, though "not a member of our Conference," would have been allowed to remain, that he, too, might be "refreshed" and instructed. It is difficult to imagine how men engaged in such HOLY work, could perpetrate so great an act of cruelty, as to turn out a brother, who was quietly waiting to listen and learn.

The Minutes, which, though repeatedly read, have not been questioned by any one, state that it was "moved that we will not allow the character of B. T. Roberts to pass, until he has had a fair trial. Passed." The Chairman does not deny that such action was had, but tells us that he does "not remember such motion." He says, "There was conversation concerning his case; and the general sentiment, so far as expressed, was, that he should have a fair trial."

Here are all the elements of a conspiracy to ruin the ministerial character of an absent brother: first, a pledge of secrecy; second, turning out one whom, they thought, could not be trusted with their secret doings; third, an expression, to give him "a fair trial," which was, doubtless, understood to mean, "we will vote for his condemnation." If this was not the understanding, how did it happen that these men stood up in a solid body against me? They alone condemned me.

If it be a sin to question the righteousness of a verdict bringing me in guilty of "immoral and unchristian conduct," for publishing what was never published—a verdict agreed upon in the secret conclave of an opposing party—I trust it is not a mortal sin. Ever since that verdict was rendered, I have thought that it was utterly wrong and wicked, admitting of no apology or palliation. I presume I shall always be of the same opinion.

The pamphlet which forms the basis of the present trial, contains the article for which I was tried last year, and another article, by George W. Estes, giving the charge and specifications, together with a short account of the trial. This latter part contains some things that I never approved of, and which I have always regretted were ever published.

I stand charged with "publishing, or assisting in the publication and circulation" of this entire document. The opposing counsel has labored earnestly to give the term "publishing" the technical signification of "making public," using many times the phrase "circulating, and thereby publishing." But this, I am certain, is not the sense in which the term was used when the charges were framed. They expected to prove that I had something to do, in some way, with publishing the document, that is, in issuing it from the press.

The phraseology of the specification must satisfy any one of this. Yet, if any doubt remains that the popular sense of the word "publishing" is the sense in which it was intended, a single fact will remove every doubt.

Since this trial was commenced, the editor of the Brockport paper, who printed the document under consideration, was sent for, by the opposite side, post-haste.

He came on as quick as he could come, changing horses by the way, but, after being closeted with the counsel, was sent back, without being called upon the stand, or any intimation being given to us that he was present. I suppose they found out the facts in the case—that I had nothing to do whatever, directly or indirectly, with publishing the pamphlet. But this makes no difference with them; they set their wits to work, and called in the help of legal technicalities.

Not only is there an utter absence of proof that I published, or assisted in publishing the document so offensive to them, but the proof is positive, that I had nothing to do with it whatever.

George W. Estes testifies that I did not publish, nor assist in publishing, or defraying the expense of publishing, the document under consideration; that I never consented to the republication of "New-School Methodism;" nor had anything to do with writing the part that bears his name; that I did not, to his knowledge, even know that its publication was intended.

This testimony is explicit; it comes from a responsible source—from a highly respected exhorter in our Church.

The only foundation that remains on which to rest the heavy charge of "immoral and unchristian conduct," is the alleged circulation of this document. Suppose the proof of circulation were ever so conclusive, this would constitute no reason why I should be put on my trial for immoral conduct, as though some great crime had been committed. Had I been permitted to go on, I should have shown that there are but few preachers in the Conference, that have not circulated it more or less. One witness testifies that he obtained twenty-six—bought some, and some were given to him—but declines to tell what he did with them.

Is he immoral? Is every one immoral that has circulated that pamphlet? No one believes it; yet no one could have as good a reason for circulating it as myself. On going to my charge, last fall, an entire stranger, I found that one of the preachers, on his way from Conference, had stopped with one of the principal families of the society with which I was appointed to labor. In answer to the usual inquiries about the new preacher, he told them that he was the one that was convicted of immoral conduct, on nine out of ten specifications.

Of course, they felt like not receiving the preacher. They could not think what they had done, that they should have one sent to them to preach the gospel who had been convicted of immoral conduct.

During the year, I was invited to preach in a church of another denomination. Before the time came for filling the appointment, our preacher, stationed in the place, called upon the pastor of the church where I was to preach, and gravely informed him that the person who was to occupy his pulpit had been convicted of immoral conduct, at the last session of the Conference.

The Buffalo *Advocate*, and the *Christian Advocate and Journal*, have published to the world, that I was found guilty of "immoral and unchristian conduct;" and, when a friend of mine sought to make an explanation, through the columns of the *Advocate and Journal*, he was refused permission. Could any thing be more natural than that I should desire to have my friends read the article for which I had been condemned, that they might judge for themselves, whether there was any thing that should occasion them to withdraw their confidence? It was, undoubtedly, a conviction of the propriety of this, that excited the unfounded suspicion that I had something to do with the republication of *New-School Methodism*.

The account which George Estes gives of the trial, is the only account that was ever published. It contains some rather sharp things; and yet there is nothing by any means as severe as may be found in the writings of John Wesley, the founder of our denomination.

Wesley says of his brethren, the clergy: "There are, among yourselves, ungodly and unholy men—openly, undeniably such—drunkards, gluttons, returners of evil for evil, liars, swearers, profaners of the day of the Lord."—Vol. v; page 24.

The Archbishop of York sent a paternal address to the clergy of his diocese. Part of it ran nearly, if not exactly, thus:

" There is great indiscretion in preaching up a sort of religion, as the true and only Christianity, which, in their own account of it, consists in an enthusiastic ardor, to be understood, or attained, by very few, and not to be practiced without breaking in upon the common duties of life."

Wesley replies to this in the following severe terms. " O, my lord, what manner of words are these! Supposing candour and love out of the question, are they the words of truth? I dare stake my life upon it, there is not one true clause in all this paragraph." P. 42. Why did not his grace have him turned out of the Church, upon a charge of libel, for accusing him of lying?

He charges some who call themselves Protestants with being worse than Bonner. " Why Edmund Bonner would have starved the heretics in prison; whereas you starved them in their own houses!" Vol. v., p. 91.

" What cobbler in London is not wiser than the principal Secretary of State? What coffee house disputer is not an abler divine than his grace of Canterbury." Vol. v., p. 121.

Of his brethren the clergy he says: "There are found among us covetous men, men "who mind earthly things," who "seek themselves" and not Christ crucified, who "love the world and the things of the world." Vol. v., p. 125. Again, "How many are there who do not study to speak what is true, especially to the rich and great, so much as what is pleasing? Who flatter honourable sinners instead of telling them plain, 'How can ye escape the damnation of hell?'" P. 127.

Of some of the clergy he says: "You it is certain have shown the utmost hatred to us, and in every possible way; unless you were actually to beat us, (of which also we are not without precedent,) or shoot us through the head; and if you could prevail upon others to do this I suppose you would think you did God service. * * * * *

It is my brethren your own preaching, and not ours which sets the people against you. The very same persons who are diverted with those sermons, cannot but despise you for them in their heart; even those who on your authority believe most of the assertions which you advance. What then must they think of you, who know the greatest part of what you assert to be utterly false? They may pity and pray for you; but they can esteem you no other than false witnesses against God and your brethren." Vol. v., p. 162.

"God begins a glorious work in our land, you set yourself against it with all your might to prevent its beginning where it does not yet appear, and to destroy it wherever it does. In part you prevail. You keep many from hearing the word that is able to save their souls. Others who had heard it you induce to turn from God, and to list under the devil's banner again. Then you make the success of your own wickedness an excuse for not acknowledging the work of God! You urge that not many sinners reformed; and that some of them are as bad as ever! Whose fault is this? Is it ours or your own? Why have not thousands more been reformed? Yea, for every one who is now turned to God, why are there not ten thousand? Because you and your associates labored too heartily in the cause of hell; because you and they spared no pains either to prevent or to destroy the work of God! By using all the power and wisdom you had, you hindered thousands from hearing the Gospel which they might have found to be the power of God unto salvation. Their blood is upon your heads. By inventing or countenancing, or retailing lies, some refined, some gross and palpable, you hindered others from profiting by what they did hear. You are answerable to God for these souls also. Many who began to taste the good word, and run the way of God's commandments, you, by various methods, prevailed on to hear it no more; so they soon drew back to perdition. But know, that for every one of these also, God will require an account of you in the day of judgment."

Wesley lived in a comparatively dark age of the world. A superstitious reverence was still felt for the priesthood, especially for its higher order. The freedom of the press was not fully established. Wesley had made himself extremely obnoxious to the ministry of his own Church. He had totally disregarded the established ways of the Church and violated her plainest canons. Yet he could scandalize the priesthood with impunity! Could tell them that there were among them "*drunkards*," "*swearers*," "*liars*," "*profaners of the day of the Lord.*" Could charge an Archbishop with writing a paragraph that did not "*contain one true clause in it.*" Could charge his brethren in the ministry with "*setting themselves with all their might against a glorious work of God.*" With "*laboring heartily in the cause of hell.* With "*inventing or countenancing, or retailing lies.*"

Of course those against whom these charges were brought did not admit their truth. Yet even in that dark age, among a ministry that we are accustomed to regard as very deficient in piety, there was too much light and too much of the spirit of Christ to attempt to put down an opponent by Ecclesiastical prosecutions, whom they could not silence by argument! Can it possible that in an age and country that boasts of the freedom of speech and of the press, the professed followers of John Wesley should exhibit a degree of intolerance, that was never manifested by his bitterest enemies in the height of their opposition?

The spirit that dictated the prosecution of last year and this, would be much more befitting a narrow minded monk of the middle age, than a Protestant Minister in the latter half of the nineteenth century.

If, then, instead of having had nothing to do whatever with the publication of the offending "document," I had actually written it, no just ground would have existed for this partizan trial.

But let us look more closely into this matter of circulation. I think it will be seen that if the document were ever so unsuitable for circulation, the testimony is totally insufficient to convict me even of that.

Rev. J. P. Kent, a friend that I trust, testified that "he asked me for one; and that I told him I *did not* circulate them, but had no objection to his seeing the one that I had."

Rev. R. Wilcox, a local deacon in our Church in Pekin, where I have labored the past year, a man with whom I have been very intimate, testifies that he "*first* saw the pamphlet after he left home on his way to Conference!" Never saw one in Pekin! This shows that I could not have been very industrious in circulating it.

The *only* witness that testifies to my having any agency in its circulation is Rev. John Bowman. His testimony is in substance as follows: "Bro. Roberts gave me a package containing three dozen of the pamphlets, on the cars between Lockport and Medina. He requested me to circulate them. He desired me to leave a portion of of them with Bro. Codd or Bro. Williams of Medina, provided I fell in company with them. I asked him whether they were to be distributed gratuitously or sold; he said he would like to get enough to defray the expenses of printing, but circulate them anyhow. He mentioned he had been at some considerable expense."

In his cross examiantion he says: "I was counsel for defendant in his trial last year. He appeared to repose confidence in me." . . . . "I told him I would take the documents and consider the case. I took them home and put them away in a by-place. . . . . About six weeks ago I lent Dr. Chamberlayne several copies."

From this testimony, supposing it to be correct—and it is all there is to prove that I had any agency in the circulation of this "document"—it does not appear that a single copy ever become public through my instrumentality. The most that can be made of it is that I *once* made an attempt to circulate it, but was unsuccessful.

But let us see what reliance, if any, is to be placed upon this testimony. The conversation he professes to relate, is alleged to have taken place soon after I was tried by this Conference, for issuing the first edition of New-School Methodism. He says he was my counsel and that I appeared to repose confidence in him. According to his own statement he was a betrayer of confidence! of confidence growing out of a professional relation; which among the most unprincipled of men is regarded as sacred! This throws suspicion over his entire testimony.

Hume, in his History of England, in relating the fact of one nobleman's accusing another in Parliament "of having spoken to him in private many slanderous words of the King," says of the accuser that he " was certainly very little delicate in the point of honor, when he revealed a private conversation to the ruin of the person who had intrusted him ; and we may thence be more inclined to believe the other's denial than his asseveration."

This is the morality of an infidel! But little reliance is to be placed upon the declaration of that man who betrays his friend! Shall the standard of morality among Christian Ministers fall below that of unbelievers? Shall we allow that the man who wantonly betrays his brother, that had honored him with his confidence, is to be unqualifiedly believed ? * His testimony should be taken at a great discount, even if it was entirely uncontradicted.

But, in one material point, it is contradicted by a witness entirely reliable. Bowman says: " Bro. Roberts mentioned that he had been at some considerable expense, in getting the document printed." That I never could have told him so, is evident from the testimony of George W. Estes, who published the pamphlet. He says that "Bro. Roberts had not, so far as he knows, any knowledge that its publication was intended ; that he never was responsible, in whole or in part, for the payment of its publication; and that he (Bro. Roberts) never, to his knowledge, contributed any thing to the expenses of its publication! " George Estes told the truth!

It is well understood that in our Church trials we are not allowed to impeach, in form, any witness who is a member of our Church, no matter how easily it might be done. The *only* impeachment that is allowed, is, to show that he has made to other persons, statements contradicting those which he has made as a witness. If this can be shown, the witness stands impeached, to all intents and purposes. His testimony is to be discredited.

Let us see how the case stands with Rev. John Bowman. When called to testify upon another point, he says, " *He cannot say that there was any threat* " made to him if he did not take back what he had said in favor of Bro. Kingsley : " We all would suffer in common, in consequence of our having an inefficient Presiding Elder." This, according to his statement as a witness, was all the consequence that another preacher said would follow to him, " personally," if he did not retract his eulogy of Bro. Kingsley.

Compare this with what he said to others, in relation to this matter.

---

* Dante, the Milton of Italy, in his Divina Comedia, divides hell into nine circles. The least guilty among the lost he places in the outer or first circle, where the punishment is slightest. The more wicked are placed in the second, and so on according to the enormity of their crimes. The ninth or last circle is reserved for the most flagitious sinners. This circle he divides into four wards ; in the inmost round of the inmost circle—the very centre of hell—exposed to the immediate torments of Satan himself—*he places those who* betrayed the confidence reposed in them by their friends. He says:

> " Fraud, that in every conscience leaves a sting,
> May be by man employed on one, whose trust
> He wins, or on another who withholds
> Strict confidence. Seems as the latter way
> Broke but the bond of love which nature makes.
>   The other way
> Forgets both Nature's general love, and that
> Which thereto added afterward gives birth
> To special faith. Whence in the lesser circle,
> Point of the universe, dread seat of Dis,
> The traitor is eternally consumed."
>   *Cary's translation, Canto xi.*

Rev. R. E. Thomas testifies that "Bro. Bowman told me that a member of the Conference said to him, if he did not take back what he had said in reference to Bro. Kingsley, on the Conference floor, he would rue it."

Rev. C. C. Church, Rev. E. S. Furman, and Rev. Wm. Barrett, all testify to the same effect as Bro. Thomas. Bro. Barrett adds, that Bro. Bowman told him, more than twenty times during the year, that he had been threatened by a member of this Conference, if he did not take back what he had said in favor of Bro. Kingsley.

We all know how much more readily we remember matters affecting us personally, than we do those which relate to others. Narrating an event frequently has, also, a strong tendency to fix it in the memory. Yet here is a threat made to Rev. John Bowman personally, which he has mentioned to four different preachers, during the year, and to one of them a score of times at least, (others might have been brought, if necessary,) and yet, when he is called to testify in relation to it, *"He cannot say that any threat was made"* to him at all! Can any reliance be placed upon a witness whose memory is so treacherous? Not the least credit would be given to such testimony in a court of justice. Such is the *only* witness* brought forward to prove my agency in the circulation of this document. Were not this testimony of so extremely doubtful character, it would still be insufficient to procure a conviction. In the Statute Book, that ought to govern in this case, we read: *"Moreover, if thy brother shall trespass against thee, go and tell him his fault between thee and him alone: if he shall hear thee, thou hast gained thy brother. But, if he will not hear thee, then take with thee one or two more, that, in the mouth of two or three witnesses, every word may be established.*—Matt., xviii, 15, 16.

This first direction has never been followed. Though the offense is charged to have been committed in the early part of the Conference year, no brother has so much as intimated that he considered himself trespassed against.

Again, we read: *"Against an Elder receive not an accusation, but before two or three witnesses."*—1 Tim., v, 19. In accordance with these plain passages, is the provision of our Discipline, which says: *"Out of the mouth of two or three witnesses, he shall be condemned."*

This, then, is the law of the Church. It requires the testimony of two or more witnesses. The language is explicit and unambiguous. *Some of the parties concerned in this prosecution, are far more deeply interested than we possibly can be, in establishing the doctrine that more than one witness is necessary to secure the conviction of an Elder.*

In this case, there is the testimony of only one witness; and that has been impeached, as fully as the testimony of a member of our Church can be impeached.

It has been urged, at great length, by the opposing counsel, that, because we went into the merits of the case, and showed that many things in the pamphlet are true, therefore we ought to be condemned, whether there is any proof that we circulated it or not. This is strange logic. We are charged with publishing, or assisting in the publication and circulation of, a certain document; and, if we are to be condemned, we

---

* The course of this witness in Conference matters reminds one of what Homer says of the treacherous God of War:

" From these to those he flies ;
And every side of wavering combat tries;
Large promise makes and breaks the promise made
Now gives the Grecians, now the Trojans aid.

insist upon it, that we ought to be first proved guilty of what has been charged against us. We protest against being condemned, because we have not conducted the defense in a manner more satisfactory to the opposing counsel. My friend, Bro. Stiles, has done nobly; I have done the best I could; and if we have, in our inexperience, committed any mistakes in the management of this case, I insist upon it, that I ought not to be brought in guilty of "immoral and unchristian conduct," on that account.*

The counsel has dwelt long and earnestly upon the aggravated nature of the offense charged. If the accusation had been for the most atrocious crime, it could not have been urged with greater vehemence and zeal. Libel is an offence that may or may not involve moral delinquency. Some of the best men in our Church have been convicted of libel—not before a partizan tribunal, but by a civil court, and mulcted in damages. The venerated Bishops, Emery, and Waugh, and Dr. Bangs, were brought in, by an impartial jury, guilty of libeling a business man, and yet they suffered no loss of confidence on that account.

But here the most strenuous exertions are put forth to make out that in the long catalogue of crime, there is none of quite so deep a dye, as the handing, to a supposed friend, of a package of pamphlets, which contain some animadversions upon a party of men, which they are pleased to consider libelous.

To the accusation which has been so repeatedly made, of my being a young man, I plead guilty. To the liability of human nature to be mistaken in judgment, I claim no exemption. But allow me to suggest, that if I have fallen into any mistakes, the best way to correct them will not be by partizan prosecutions, under frivolous pretexts. Their tendency will rather be to create the suspicion that my position is one that could not be successfully assailed by argument. Convince me that I am wrong, and you shall find no man more ready to confess it, and more willing to be set right.

Finally, brethren, allow me to say that I do not affect any indifference as to the results of this investigation. I have an ardent attachment for the Church of my choice. I love her doctrines, her usages, and her aggressive spirit. If I have erred at all, it has been occasioned by loving the Church too much, rather than too little. Any departure from the landmarks of Methodism has awakened jealous solicitude, and called forth whatever influence I possessed, to persuade our people to "ask for the old paths, that they might walk therein." It has been my offense not to have labored altogether in vain. We have been favored by the Great Head of the Church, with revivals, deep and powerful, such as have given to our beloved Zion her present position among the Churches of the Lord.

It would be our delight to continue to toil in the same blessed work, with what little ability and energy the Lord has been pleased to endow us with. This, above all others, is the service that I delight in, and to which I feel God has specially called and commissioned me from on high. I do not feel that my work is done, nor my commission from the Lord revoked. I love the Methodist Episcopal Church; no one has

---

* Since the trial I learn that some who voted against me, attempt to rescue themselves on the ground that we attempted a vindication of the statements of the pamphlets. They say if we had made no defence we would have been acquitted. Yet these same men voted against us last year when we did not examine a single witness! We attempted the examination of only one. If this information be correct it would seem that I was convicted of "unchristian and immoral conduct," not for "publishing and circulating" the pamphlet, but for attempting to bring to light the secret doings of the Regency party !

ever heard me say aught against her; and I should esteem it my highest privilege to be permitted to put forth mightier efforts than I have ever done, to build up her walls and enlarge her borders.

We are hastening to a great, impartial tribunal, before which all actions must pass in review, and all secrets be revealed. There the deliberations of this hour, and the motives by which we are governed, will be disclosed before an assembled universe. Remember it is written: "WITH WHAT JUDGMENT YE JUDGE, YE SHALL BE JUDGED; AND WITH WHAT MEASURE YE METE, IT SHALL BE MEASURED UNTO YOU AGAIN."

APPENDIX.

NEW SCHOOL METHODISM.

The best seed sown, from year to year, on poor soil, gradually degenerates. The acorn, from the stately oak, planted upon the arid plain, becomes a stinted shrub. Ever since the fall, the human heart has proved a soil unfavorable to the growth of truth.

Noxious weeds flourish everywhere spontaneously, while the useful grains require diligent cultivation.

Correct principles implanted in the mind need constant attention, or monstrous errors will overtop them and root them out. Every old nation tells the tale of her own degeneracy, and points to the golden age when truth and justice reigned among men.

Religious truth is not exempt from this liability to corruption. "God will take care of his own cause," is a maxim often quoted by the cowardly and the compromising, as an apology for their base defection. When His servants are faithful to the trusts reposed in them, it is gloriously true; when they waver, His cause suffers. The Churches planted by the Apostles, and watered by the blood of martyrs, now outvie heathenism itself in their corruptions. No other parts of the world are so inaccessible ; to gospel truth as those countries where the Romish and Greek Churches hold dominion.

As a denomination, we are just as liable to fall by corrupting influences, as any were that have flourished before us. We enjoy no immunity from danger. Already there is springing up among us a class of preachers whose teaching is very different from that of the fathers of Methodism. They may be found here and there throughout our Zion; but in the Genesee Conference they act as an associate body. They number about thirty. During the last session of this Conference, they held several secret meetings, in which they concerted a plan to carry their measures and spread their doctrines. They have openly made the issue in the Conference. It is divided. Two distinct parties exist. With the one or the other every preacher is in sympathy. This difference is fundamental. It does not relate to things indifferent, but to those of the most vital importance. It involves nothing less than the nature itself of Christianity.

In showing the doctrines of the New School Methodists, we shall quote from the *The Advocate* of the sect, published at Buffalo. This is the organ of the party. It is sustained by them. They act as its agents. Where their influence prevails, it is circulated to the exclusion of other religious papers. Its former title was " *The Buffalo*

Christian Advocate." But since its open avowal of the new doctrines, it has signifi-
cantly dropped from its caption, the expressive word "*Christian.*" This omission is
full of meaning. It is, however, highly proper, as we shall see when we examine its
new theory of religion. We commend the editor for this instance of honesty. It is
now simply "*The Advocate ;*" that is, the *only* Advocate of the tenets it defends.

The New School Methodists affect as great a degree of liberalism as do Theodore
Parker and Mr. Newman. They possess "charity" for everybody except their brethren of the Old School. In an article on "Creeds," published in *The Advocate* of April
16th, under the signature of W. the Rev. writer, a prominent New School minister,
lays it on to "the sects whose watchword is a creed," in a manner not unworthy of
Alexander Campbell himself. He says, "No matter how holy and blameless a man's
life may be, if he has the temerity to question any tenet of 'orthodoxy,' he is at once,
in due ecclesiastical form, consigned to the Devil—as a heretic and infidel. Thus are
the fetters of a spiritual despotism thrown around the human reason. * * * And
so it has come to pass, that in the estimation of multitudes—the teachings of Paul are
eclipsed by the theories of Calvin, and the writings of John Wesley are held in higher
veneration than the inspired words of St. John." Is not that a modest charge ?

But their theory of religion is more fully set forth in the leading editorial of *The
Advocate* for May 14th, under the title—" *Christianity a religion of beneficence rather than
of devotion.*" Though it appears as editorial, we have good reason to believe that it
was written by a leading New School member of the Genesee Conference. It has not
been disavowed by that party. Though it has been before the public for months, no
one has expressed a dissent from its positions. It is fair to suppose that it represents
the views of the leaders of this new movement.

It says, " Christianity is not characteristically a system of devotion. *It has none of
those features* which must distinguish a religion grounded on the idea, that to adore the
divine character is the most imperative obligation resting upon human beings. It
enjoins the observance of but very few sacred rites ; nor does it prescribe any *particular mode* for paying homage to the Deity. It eschews all exterior forms, and
teaches that they who worship God must worship Him in spirit and in truth."

The Old School Methodists hold, that "to adore the Divine character" is the most
imperative obligation resting upon human beings—that Christianity has *all* of those
features that must distinguish religion grounded on this idea. That he who worships
God rightly, will, as a necessary consequence, possess all social and moral virtues ;
that the gospel does not leave its votaries to choose, if they please, the degrading rites
of heathenism, or the superstitious abominations of Popery ; but prescribes prayer and
praise and the observance of the sacraments of baptism and the Lord's Supper, "as
particular modes of paying homage to the Deity ;" that there is no necessity for antag-
onism, as Infidels and Unversalists are wont to affirm, between spiritual worship and
the forms of worship instituted by Christ.

The following sneer is not unworthy of Thomas Paine himself. It falls below the
dignity of Voltaire. "Christianity in nowise gives countenance to the supposition,
that the Great Jehovah is so affected with the infirmity of vanity, as to receive with
peculiarly grateful emotions, the attention and offerings which poor human creatures
may pay directly to Him in worship."

The above may be sufficient to show what Christianity is not, in the opinion of these
New School divines. Let us now see what it is. "The characteristic idea of this
system is benevolence ; and its practical realization is achieved in beneficence. It

consecretes the principle of charity, and instructs its votaries to regard good works as the holiest sacrifice, and the most acceptable which they can bring to the Almighty.

* * * * * * * * *

"Whatever graces may be necessary to constitute the inner Christian life, the chief and principal one of these, is *love to man.* * * * The great condition upon which one becomes a participant of the gospel salvation, is—some practical exhibition of self-abnegation, of self-sacrifice for the good of others. *Go sell all that thou hast, and give to the poor,* were the only terms of salvation which Christ proposed to the young man who, otherwise, was not far from the kingdom of heaven."

The Old School Methodists hold that benevolence is only *one of the fruits* of true religion, but by no means the thing itself. In their view, "The principal grace of the inner Christian life" is LOVE TO GOD, and "the most acceptable sacrifice we can render HIM, is a broken and contrite heart. They teach that the great condition upon which one becomes "a participant of the gospel salvation" IS FAITH IN CHRIST—preceded by repentance. They read in the gospel that the young man referred to, was commanded by Christ to "*come, take up the cross and follow me.*" The giving of his goods to the poor was only preparatory to this.

The New School Methodists hold that justification and entire sanctification, or holiness, are the same—that when a sinner is pardoned, he is at the same time made holy—that all the spiritual change he may henceforth expect, is simply a growth in grace. When they speak of "holiness," they mean by it the same as do evangelical ministers of those denominations which do not receive the doctrines taught by Wesley and Fletcher on this subject.

According to the Old School Methodists, merèly justified persons, while they do not outwardly commit sin, are conscious of sin still remaining in the heart, such as pride, self-will, and unbelief. They continually feel a heart bent to back-sliding; a natural tendency to evil; a proneness to depart from God, and cleave to the things of earth. Those that are sanctified wholly are saved from all inward sin—from evil thoughts, and evil tempers. No wrong temper, none contrary to love remains in the soul. All the thoughts, words and actions are governed by pure love.

The New School ministers have the frankness to acknowledge that their doctrines are not the doctrines of the Church. They have undertaken to correct the teachings of her standard authors. In the same editorial of "The Advocate," from which we have quoted so largely, we read: "So in the exercises and means of grace instituted by the Church, it is clearly apparent that respect is had, rather to the excitation of the religious sensibilities, and the culture of emotional piety, than the developement of genial and humane dispositions, and the formation of habits of active, vigorous goodness."

Here the evils complained of are charged upon "*the exercises and means of grace, instituted by the Church.*" They do not result from a perversion of the means of grace, but are the effects *intended* to be produced in their institution. It is THE CHURCH, then, that is wrong—and so far wrong that she does not even *aim* at the development of proper Christian character. "The means of grace," in the use of which an Asbury, an Olin, a Hedding, and a host of worthies departed and living, were nurtured to spiritual manhood, must be abolished; and others adapted to the "development of genial and humane dispositions," established in their place. The lodge must supersede the class and the love feast; and the old fashioned prayer meeting must give way to the social party! Those who founded or adopted "the exercises and means of grace instituted by the Church"—Paul and Peter, the Martyrs, and Reformers, Luther and Wesley, Calvin and Edwards—all have failed to comprehend the true idea of Christianity—for these all held that the sinner was justified by *Faith in Christ*, and not by "some practical exhibition of self-abnegation." The honor of distinctly apprehending and clearly stating the true genius of Christianity, was reserved for a few divines of the nineteenth century!

In our next we shall show the usages and the results, so far as developed, of New School Methodism.

USAGES—RESULTS.

Differing thus in their views of religion, the Old and New School Methodists necessarily differ in their measures for its promotion. The latter build stock churches, and furnish them with pews to accommodate a select congregation; and with organs, melodeons, violins, and professional singers, to execute difficult pieces of music for a fashionable audience. The former favor free churches, congregational singing, and spirituality, simplicity and fervency in worship. They endeavor to promote revivals deep and thorough; such as were common under the labors of the Fathers; such as have made Methodism the leading denomination of the land. The leaders of the New Divinity movement are not remarkable for promoting revivals; and those which do, occasionally, occur among them, may generally be characterized as the editor of " *The Advocate*" designated one which fell under his notice, as "*splendid revivals.*" Preachers of the old stamp urge upon all who would gain heaven, the necessity of self-denial —non-conformity to the world; purity of heart and holiness of life; while the others ridicule singularity, encourage by their silence, and in some cases by their own example, and that of their wives and daughters, " the putting on of gold and costly apparel," and treat with distrust all professions of deep Christian experience. When these desire to raise money for the benefit of the Church, they have resource to the selling of pews to the highest bidder; to parties of pleasure, oyster suppers, fairs, grab bags, festivals and lotteries; the others, for this purpose, appeal to the love the people bear to Christ. In short, the Old School Methodists rely for the spread of the gospel upon the agency of the Holy Ghost and the purity of the Church. The New School Methodists appear to depend upon the patronage of the worldly, the favor of the proud and aspiring; and the various artifices of worldly policy.

If this diversity of opinion and of practice among the ministers of our denomination, was confined to one Conference, it would be comparatively unimportant. But unmistakable indications show that prosperity is producing upon us, as a denomination, the same intoxicating effect, that it too often does upon individuals and societies. The change, by the General Conference of 1852, in the rule of Discipline, requiring that all our houses of worship should be built plain, and with free seats; and that of the last General Conference in the section respecting dress, show that there are already too many among us, who would take down the barriers that have hitherto separated us from the world. The fact that the removal is gradual, so as not to excite too much attention and commotion, renders it none the less alarming.

Every lover of the Church must feel a deep anxiety to know what is to be the result of this new order of things. If we may judge by its effects in the Genesee Conference, since it has held sway there, it will prove disastrous to us as a denomination. It so happened, either by accident, or by management, at the division of the Genesee Conference, eight years ago, that most of the unmanageable veterans, who could neither be induced to depart from the Heaven honored usages of Methodism, by the specious cry of "progress," nor to wink at such departures, by the mild expostulations of Eli, "Why do you thus my son!" had their destination upon the east side of Genesee River. The first year after the division, the East Genesee Conference had twenty superannuated preachers; the Genesee Conference but five. "Men of progress" in the prime of life, went west of the river, and took possession of the Conference. For the most part, they have borne sway there ever since. Of late, the young men of the Conference, uniting with the fathers, and thus united, comprising a majority of the Conference, have endeavored to stop this "progress" away from the old path of Methodism. But the "progressives" make up in management what they lack in numbers. Having free access at all times to the ears of the Episcopacy, they have succeeded, for the most part, in controlling the appointments to the Districts and most important stations. If, by reason of his obvious fitness, any impracticable adherent of primitive Methodism has been appointed to a district or first class station, he has usually been pursued, with untiring diligence, and hunted from his position before his constitutional term expired.

In the bounds of the Genesee Conference, the people generally are pre-possessed in favor of Methodism. During the past eight years there have been no external causes operating there against our prosperity, that do not operate at all times and in all places. Within this period, the nominal increase of the Church in that Conference has been but seven hundred and eighty. The East Genesee Conference has had an increase, within the same time, of about two thousand five hundred. In order to have simply kept place with the population, there should have been within the bounds of the Genesee Conference, one thousand six hundred and forty-three more members than there are at present. That is, in eight years, under the reign of New Divinity, the Church has suffered, within the bounds of this one Conference, a relative loss of fifteen per cent. in members.

The Seminary at Lima, at the time of the division, second to none in the land, has, by the same kind of management, been brought to the brink of financial ruin.

We have thus endeavored to give a fair and impartial representation of New School Methodism. Its prevalence in one Conference has already, as we have seen, involved it in division and disaster. Let it generally prevail, and the glory will depart from Methodism. She has a special mission to accomplish. This is, not to gather into her fold the proud and fashionable, the devotees of pleasure and ambition, but, "to spread scripture holiness over these lands." Her doctrines, and her usages, her hymns, her history, and her spirit, her noble achievements in the past, and her bright prospects for the future, all forbid that she should adopt an accommodating, compromising policy, pandering to the vices of the times. Let her go on, as she has done, insisting that the great cardinal truths of the gospel shall receive a living embodiment in the hearts and lives of her members, and Methodism will continue to be the favored of Heaven, and the joy of the earth. But let her come down from her position, and receive to her communion all those lovers of pleasure, and lovers of the world, who are willing to pay for the privilege, and it needs no prophet's vision to foresee that Methodism will become a dead and corrupting body, endeavoring in vain to supply, by the erection of splendid Churches, and the imposing performance of powerless ceremonies, the manifested glory of the Divine presence, which once shone so brightly in all her sanctuaries.

"*Thus saith the Lord, stand ye in the ways and see, and ask for the old paths, where is the good way, and walk therein, and ye shall find rest for your souls.*" R.

TO WHOM IT MAY CONCERN.

THE foregoing article in the *Northern Independent* was made the subject of general consultations, in private caucuses of the Buffalo Regency, held in a room over Bryant & Clark's book-store, at Le Roy, on Thursday, Friday, and Saturday evenings, of the first week of the Conference; the result of which was the Bill of Charges given below. The manner of committing the feebler of the preachers to the condemnation of Bro. Roberts in advance, was on this wise, as related by one present: One of the chiefs of the Regency, acting as Chairman, asked: "What shall be done in the case of Bro. Roberts? All in favor of his prosecution raise your hands!" The "immortal thirty" raised their hands, and a few presiding elderlings. The Chairman then delivered a flaming exhortation to unanimity—that they must be united enough *to carry the matter through*, or it would not do to undertake it. After sundry exhortations, the vote was taken again, and a few more voted. After another season of fervent exhortation, a third vote was taken, in which all, save one, concurred; and the trial and condemnation were determined upon. Beautiful work this for godly Methodist preachers, deriving their support from honest religious societies among us! We put their Bill of Charges, with all its ingenious distortion of facts, on record, here before the people, as follows:

"CHARGE AGAINST REV. B. T. ROBERTS.

"I hereby charge Rev. B. T. Roberts with unchristian and immoral conduct.

"1. In publishing, in the *Northern Independent*, that there exists, in the Genesee Conference, an associate body, numbering about thirty, whose teaching is very different from that of the fathers of Methodism.

"2. In publishing, as above, that said members of Genesee Conference are opposed to what is fundamental in Christianity — to the nature itself of Christianity.

"3. In classing them, in the above-mentioned publication, with Theodore Parker and Mr. Newman, as regards laxness of religious sentiment.

"4. In charging them, as above, with sneering at Christianity in a manner not unworthy of Thomas Paine, and that falls below that of Voltaire.

"5. In charging them, as above, with being heterodox on the subject of holiness.

"6. In asserting that they acknowledge that their doctrines are not the doctrines of the Church, and that they have undertaken to correct the teachings of her standard authors.

"7. In charging them, as above, with attempting to abolish the means of grace — substituting the lodge for the class-meeting and love-feast, and the social party for the prayer-meeting.

"8. In representing, as above, the revivals among them as superficial, and characterizing them as "splendid revivals."

"9. In saying, as above, that they treat with distrust all professions of deep religious experience.

"Le Roy, September 1, 1857.   REUBEN C. FOOTE."

For several years past, there has been the annual sacrifice of a human victim at the Conference. It has become a custom. The religious rites and ceremonies attending this annual lustration assume a legal complexion. The victim is immolated according to law. E. Thomas, J. McCreery, C. Kingsley, L. Stiles, and B. T. Roberts, constitute the "noble band of martyrs" thus far. Who is selected for the next annual victim is not yet known. The midnight conclave of the "immortal thirty" has not yet made its selection. No man is safe who dares even whisper a word against this secret inquisition in our midst. Common crime can command its indulgences; bankruptcies and adulteries are venial offenses; but opposition to its schemes and policies is a "mortal sin" — a crime "without benefit of clergy." The same fifty men who voted Bro. Roberts guilty of "unchristian and immoral conduct," for writing the above article, voted to readmit a brother from the regions round about Buffalo, for the service performed of kissing a young lady in the vestibule of the Conference room, during the progress of Bro. Roberts' trial. "Nero fiddled, while the martyrs burned."

Bro. Roberts' trial (if it deserves the name of trial) was marked by gross iniquity of proceedings. There are no regular church canons in the Methodist Episcopal Church, to govern the specific manner of conducting trials. All is indefinite. A glorious incertitude and independence of all legal regulations prevail. The presidential discretion must of necessity have large latitude and range, either high or low, as prejudice or policy may incline. Thus, when a witness was asked if he knew of a private meeting of about thirty preachers, at Medina, during Conference, he answered, "Yes." When asked for what purpose they met, he answered, for "consultation." Here the prosecution, perceiving that all this secret caucusing at the Medina Conference, to lock out the prayer-meetings, arrange the appointments, oust out presiding elders, etc., etc., were likely to be brought out, objected to all the questions in the case, which were not exactly covered by the verbal terms of the specifications which *they themselves* had artfully framed; and their objections were sustained by the Bishop. Every question as to the meetings of the "immortal thirty," their doings and teachings, was objected to, and ruled out, as irrelevant to the specifications.

Having been charged for affirming the existence of an associate body, of about thirty preachers, in the Conference, for purposes indicated in his article, he was denied to elicit the facts in justification, which he could have proved by thirty witnesses. This right, which any civil or military court would have allowed him, was denied. Of course where witnesses refuse to testify, and the judge refuses to compel them to do so, there was no use wasting time in defense. Bro. Roberts refused to continue the defense.

Also, a commission to take testimony was sent to Buffalo. But, when they arrived, they found an emmissary from the Conference had been sent on before them to take charge of the *Advocate* office, who refused to sell or lend, or suffer to be transcribed, any of the copy of the papers, or article, bearing on the case, and who put everybody "on the square," to refuse testimony. Having no power to compel witnesses to testify, the committee returned with such testimony only as honest men voluntarily offered, which will be hereafter published.

A venerable doctor of divinity read the "auto-da-fe" sermon, (prepared for the victim of the previous year,) wherein he consigned, in true inquisitorial style, Bro. Roberts, body and soul, to hell. This was done in his most masterly manner, evincing no embarrassing amount of idiosyncracy, or other mental cause for superannuation. This venerable D. D., though nominally superannuated, and an annual claimant of high rate upon the Conference funds, is, nevertheless, quite efficient in embarrassing effective preachers in their work, by concocting "bills of information" and "bills of charges," and pleading them to hell, for the crime of preaching and writing the truth. Whether his plea will enhance the amount of the superannuated collections for the coming year, remains to be seen.

It was moved that the vote in Bro. Roberts' case, should be taken by yeas and nays; but the same spirit of concealment, and dread of light, fostered by secret society associations, prevailed here also. Like some in the olden time, they "feared the people," and voted down the motion. The vote to sustain the charge of "unchristian and immoral conduct," for writing and publishing these strictures on New-school Methodism, was fifty-two to forty-three; being a majority of nine. Several members of Conference were absent, and several dodged, through fear of the presiding-elder influence upon their appointments.

The following preachers, as near as can be ascertained, voted to sustain the charge: I. Chamberlayne, G. Lanning, E. C. Sandborn, H. May, D. Nichols, M. Seager, R. C. Foot, G. Fillmore, A. D. Wilbor, P. Woodworth, R. L. Waite, H. Butlin, S. M. Hopkins, E. E. Chambers, G. W. Terry, J. Latham, H. W. Annis, Z. Hurd, T. Carlton, J. M. Fuller, W. H. Depuy, D. F. Parsons, S. Hunt, J. B. Lanckton, J. McEwen, H. R. Smith, S. C. Smith, G. Smith, L. Packard, C. S. Baker, W. S. Tuttle, J. McClelland, J. G. Miller, J. N. Simpkin, S. Y. Hammond, A. P. Ripley, H. M. Ripley, M. W. Ripley, E. L. Newman, A. Plumley, B. F. McNeil, R. S. Moran, E. M. Buck, J. J. Roberts, S. Parker, F. W. Conable, J. B. Wentworth, S. H. Baker, J. Timmerman, K. D. Nettleton, G. Delamater, W. C. Willing.

Another significant fact was apparent in the case—the power of the presiding eldership. Quite a number of preachers would not vote at all. Too honest to aid the conspiracy, and too cowardly to face the "loaves and fishes" argument presented by the presiding-elder influence, they sat still, and saw the condemnation of the innocent, when they might have prevented it.

The influence of the book concern had its effect upon the case. It has become a maxim in politics, "that the debtor votes the creditor's ticket." So, some indebted to the concern, discreetly refrained from voting at all; while two preachers, having refused to attend the private caucusses of the conspirators, and to pledge themselves in advance to vote for the condemnation of Bro. Roberts, were scandalized with a public report of delinquency, in open Conference, by the book agent.

But it was the influence of the slavery question which was paramount in the case. The episcopacy is understood to be conservative on that subject, and to "refer to it judicially in all the chief appointments." Hence, the Buffalo regency, in these days, notwithstanding high professions lately to the contrary, on the eve of election of delegates to the late general Conference, is also eminently conservative on that subject, and must need commend itself to the central episcopal sympathy, by great zeal against the *Northern Independent*. Its associate editor, in this Conference, must be *black-washed* in revenge, for the temerity of the people, in subscribing for the paper. They could not wreak their vengeance on the people, except by proscribing one acknowledged, above all others in the Conference, to be the PEOPLE'S MAN.

The infamous Brockport Resolutions against the Nazarites, were tacitly endorsed by the Conference, in its refusal to entertain the question of official administration, involved in their passage. This is their reward for their spaniel loyalty to the *Northern Advocate*, and every other thing that wears the label of "law and order," affixed by a pro-slavery administration. It is stated that two or three Nazarites voted with the regency, against the publication of the slavery report in the *Independent*. Surely, it must be true of them, as reported, that they court persecutions, and rejoice in being killed off at every Conference. Their strong hold upon the popular mind can not long survive their further blinking the slavery issue. We shall see.

So, brethren, in the membership of the Genesee Conference, you see we have a clique among us, called the Buffalo Regency, conspiring and acting in secret conclave, to kidnap or drive away, or proscribe and destroy, by sham trials, and starvation appointments, every one who has boldness to question their supremacy in the Conference. By threats of insubordination, and farcical outcries of strife and division, they frighten the episcopacy to give them the presiding eldership power, with its patronage of appointments; and, having that, of course they command the Conference vote, so far as they dare for fear of the people. We are fast losing our best men. The fearless champions of true Methodism are being cloven down, one after another, in our sight; and we sit loyally still, and weep and pray, and pay our money, yet another, and another year, hoping the thing will come to an end.

A thousand of us asked the Bishop to rid us of this incubus, which is crushing us into the earth. "We will do the best we can," is the stereotyped reply to our loyal entreaties. How many more victims must be immolated, how many societies must be desolated, while the episcopacy is making up its mind to grapple this monster power, which is writhing its slimy folds around the Church of God, and crushing out its life? The episcopacy, which alone has the power, having failed to redress our grievances, and rid us of this unmethodistic and foreign dynasty, there is no remedy but an appeal to personal rights. The remedy of every member is within his own reach. For one, I shall apply that remedy. For me, while looking on those preachers standing to be counted (no wonder they objected to the yeas and nays) in the vote to condemn Bro. Roberts, at Le Roy, I made up my mind that not one of them — preacher, presiding elder, or superannuated—should ever receive a cent of my money, on any pretense, or by any combination whatsoever. I shall punctually attend church at my own meeeting-house — prayer-meetings, class-meetings, love-feasts, and all the means of grace; but, if one of those men come there to preach — I can't help that; that is not my business. But I shall neither run a step, nor pay a cent. And if, as has been told, all the domestic missionary appropriations in this Conference are varied from year to year—made and withheld to suit the pockets of Regency men appointed to them—this, as long as it continues, will absolve me from obligations to that cause; the same of the superannuated fund, so long as it is controlled by that dynasty. I agreed to support the Methodist Episcopal Church as a church of the living God, not as the mere adjunct of a secular or political clique.

GEO. W. ESTES.

DOCUMENTS OF THE BUFFALO REGENCY.

We give the following extracts from articles written by leading men of the Regency party, that their tone and spirit may be compared with those documents, the circulation of which has been pronounced "unchristian and immoral conduct."

CONCERNING BISHOP HAMLIN.

"An article is going the rounds of the papers which states that Bishop Hamlin has donated $25,000 to a Western College. We don't believe a word of it. He who was once Bishop, is, if we are correctly informed, as snug and keen in the management of his finances as any other property famed man. He may have given something, nevertheless."—*The Advocate, April 12th, 1855, Editorial.*

After several efforts from the friends of the Bishop to have the above corrected, the Editor finally admitted he stood corrected, that the Bishop had given the above sum, and added the sneer, "Noble man! he shall have all our praise, if it will do him any good."

Other articles reflecting still more severely upon the Bishop have been published in *The Advocate.*

Bishop Hamlin was eminent for the advocacy of the doctrine of holiness. We can conceive of no other reason for the repeated thrusts made at him in *The Advocate.*

The following letter published in *The Advocate* of Aug. 9th, 1855, was said by the editor at the Conference for 1857, "to have been written by the man who now preaches at the first M. E. Church in Western New York." We give the letter as published *verbatim et literatim, et punctuatim.*

"mistur Edditur,
               i thought i would rite a few lines tu you tu see if you cood tell me enything about the sekt kalled by themsels, i think, NASSURRHEIGHTES, as i am too much ignorant, (which you will plees exkus) about thair proceedings, if thay ar a deesent pepul, i want to join in with them, the peepul out this way ar ful of pryd and

foller the fashions tu much; so that i want tu find, a plane peepul which don't like narrow brimmed hats, and buttons on the behind parts of the men's koats; also the tremmynges of the wimmens sleeves, and uther parts of thair dresses tu numerous to menshun, i also want to join a peepul which dont blakguard thair naburs behind thair baks. also, one which is open and free tu eneboddy. if the Nassurrheightes have eny sekrets and ar afrayd tu expose them, i wont join them; but if not, i will, no doubt, providin thay ar charetable and sweete in thair speeret and kondukt tu them which differs from thair noshuns.

> Dated in Skerystville the fyrst day
> of August of this present yeare
> JACOB SPROUT, The Reformer."

The article from which the following extracts were taken first appeared in the Medina Tribune—thence it was copied into a Universalist paper—accompanied with a eulogy of the writer, who was said by the editor to be "one of the most talented ministers in the Genesee Conference."

"NAZARITE REFORMERS AND REFORMATION."

* * * "Spurious reformers are as plenty as blackberries and as contemptable as plenty." * * They go forth before the world putting on strange and uncouth airs, which they expect everybody will regard as proof of the "divine fury" with which they are possessed, and repeating nonsensical and clap-trap phrases which they have mistakingly selected as the watchmen of a reformatory movement. The ridiculous figure they cut excites the laughter and jeers of all—save those who are as addled and silly as themselves."

* * "We, of the Genesee Conference, have such a batch of false prophets—such pseudo reformers among us. And such a group of regenators as the Nazarites compose, we cannot believe was ever before brought together by the force of a common belief in a divine call to a great work." * * "They probably felt the motion of something within them—it may have been wind in the stomach—and mistook it for the intimations of a heaven-divined commission, summoning them to the rescue of expiring Methodism, and the inauguration of a new era of spiritual life in the history of the Wesleyan movement." * * * "What fruit of transcendant godliness do they exhibit? Their *professions* indeed are loud and pretentious; but what of their works? Does holiness display itself in spiritual pride, in arrogant boastings of goodness, in canting and crabbed long facedness, in gross and filthy vituperation? In that case the palm of excellence must indeed be yielded to them."

* * "In fact, they have not yet emerged from under the Old Dispensation. To them, religion still appears to be a system of outward forms and symbols, of animal influence, and nervous sensation. With them, a long face and sanctimonious airs answer for inward purity and goodness of heart. In their creed, a high-sounding profession takes precedence of a holy life, and getting happy in a religious meeting is laid down as an indubitable proof of the Divine Favor." * * *

"They consider plainness in dress of greater moment than uprightness of character. An ornamental ribbon or flower upon a lady's bonnet is—in their eyes—an enormity greater than the sin of lying; and the wearing a ring or bracelet they think is more dangerous and damning than covetousness or slander. And generally, they preach with more powerful vehemence against superfluity in outward apparel, than against the breach of the Ten Commandments. With them, a broad-brimmed, bell-crowned hat is equivalent to the "helmet of salvation," and a shad-bellied coat to the "robe of righteousness."   JUNIUS."

www.ingramcontent.com/pod-product-compliance
Lightning Source LLC
Chambersburg PA
CBHW020518030426
42337CB00011B/444